THE GOAL OF MY LIFE

PAUL HENDERSON

WITH ROGER LAJOIE

THE GOAL OF MY LIFE

A MEMOIR

FOREWORD BY RON ELLIS

FENN
M&S

Library and Archives Canada Cataloguing in Publication

Henderson, Paul, 1943-
The goal of my life / Paul Henderson, Roger Lajoie.

ISBN 978-0-7710-4650-6

1. Henderson, Paul, 1943-. 2. Hockey players – Canada – Biography. I. Lajoie, Roger, 1958–. II. Title.

GV848.5.H4H45 2012   796.962092   C2012-900965-2

We acknowledge the financial support of the Government of Canada through the Canada Book Fund and that of the Government of Ontario through the Ontario Media Development Corporation's Ontario Book Initiative. We further acknowledge the support of the Canada Council for the Arts and the Ontario Arts Council for our publishing program.

Published simultaneously in the United States of America by Fenn/McClelland & Stewart, a division of Random House of Canada Limited, P.O. Box 1030, Plattsburgh, New York 12901

Library of Congress Control Number: 2012932349

Typeset in Sabon by M&S, Toronto
Printed and bound in the United States of America

Fenn/McClelland & Stewart, a division of Random House of Canada Limited
One Toronto Street
Suite 300
Toronto, Ontario
M5C 2V6
www.mcclelland.com

1   2   3   4   5   16   15   14   13   12

CONTENTS

FOREWORD RON ELLIS

ON MARCH 3, 1968, THE TORONTO MAPLE LEAFS traded all-star left-winger Frank Mahovlich to the Detroit Red Wings, along with forwards Pete Stemkowski and Garry Unger and the rights to defenceman Carl Brewer. In return, the Leafs got the services of Norm Ullman and Floyd Smith, both of whom were NHL veterans, and a young, up-and-coming star by the name of Paul Henderson. This was the first major trade I had witnessed in my career that involved teammates who had become close friends, reminding me that professional sport is a business. Little did I know at the time how this trade would affect the rest of my life.

In my first three seasons with the Leafs, I had lined up for faceoffs against Henderson many nights. He was fast – he could reach full speed in two strides – and he possessed an enviable snap shot that he used effectively coming off the left wing as a right-hand shot. It was obvious to me that I couldn't give him a lot of room on the ice. After Henny joined the Leafs, he said, "Well, at least I won't be shadowed by that

Ellis guy anymore." By the start of the 1968–69 season, we had become the best of friends, and so had our wives. We enjoyed many holidays in Florida together as couples after the rigours of long hockey seasons.

A major break in my career occurred when Leafs coach Punch Imlach inserted me on the right side of a line with Normie and Henny, and over the better part of six years we were known to the fans as the HUE Line. It was a pleasure going to work every day knowing that I would be sharing the ice with friends. Even though the Leafs failed to reach the upper echelon in the league standings, our line was as productive as any in the league; each of us tallied more than 150 goals between the trade and the end of the 1973–74 season. Paul led in goals, though I would have gotten closer to him if he hadn't gotten in the way one night. While I wound up to shoot the puck into an open net, Henny slid across the goal crease after being tripped and took the puck on the chin, breaking his jaw. I didn't get the goal, and Paul had to wear a cage for the rest of the season. Sorry, buddy!

Henny radiated confidence in his abilities, which was the opposite of his linemate, who was always dealing with self-doubt. His encouragement helped me through more than one scoring slump, and this wonderful character trait carried into his life after hockey. It always amazed me when he would come into the locker room before a game and quietly tell me he was going to notch a couple that night. More times than not, he'd do it. Normie and I would be the beneficiaries, picking up a few points as well.

There was a major buzz in the hockey world in the spring of 1972 around the proposed Summit Series between the

Soviet Union and Canada. The Russians were dominating international hockey at the time, and the only defence Canadian fans had was the fact that our professionals were not playing. The general consensus was that our best Canadian pros would give the Russians a thumping.

As the HUE Line was clicking on all cylinders, to our delight Henny and I got an invitation to the Team Canada training camp being held in Toronto that August. The selection committee also decided to choose Bobby Clarke, a young centre from the Philadelphia Flyers on the verge of breaking out as a star, and on the first day of camp assigned him to play between Henny and me. Clarke's style of play was very similar to Norm Ullman's, and as a result Paul and I didn't have to make adjustments to our game. To my mind, this is the main reason our line impressed and played all eight games of the series as a unit.

All of Canada remembers the shock of game one on a September evening in Montreal as we were handed a 7–3 loss. Early in the first period, when we held a 2–0 lead, Henny said to me after a shift on the ice, "This is going to be a long, long series." How right he was. The Russians were dancing and we were sucking air. This initial setback, however, set the scene for a great Canadian comeback and the heroics of my friend and teammate Paul Henderson. The script that followed was so unbelievable that Hollywood would probably have turned it down. With thirty-four seconds left on the clock in game eight, Paul Henderson scored the goal that was heard around the world. Team Canada won the Summit Series with a 4–3–1 record. Henny scored the winning goal in the final three games in Moscow, which we won 3–2, 4–3, and 6–5. Yes, we really thumped those

Russians! I was so proud of my friend, and being able to experience this life event together with him was magic.

A story came out of the winning goal, and it changes somewhat depending on who is telling it. Before the final game, Henny said to me in the locker room, "I think you are going to get the winner tonight." As noted, he was pretty good with his predictions, but I proved him wrong this time. You see, he actually scored the "Goal of the Century." No doubt about it, I got the best of him . . . I think.

In September 1973, before the Leafs training camp, we decided to take our wives for a holiday in Switzerland using the Air Canada tickets that were a gift from the series. We had a super time driving around, catching all the sights while breaking bread and sipping wine together at our various stops around the country. This holiday also started a new journey in life for all four of us.

It was decided that I would be the main driver and that Henny would be responsible for reading the maps – and unfortunately also be responsible for looking after the plane tickets. The guy who scored the Goal of the Century misread the time of departure, and as a result we missed our return flight. To top it off, Paul had to dole out some cash to put his wife, Nora, on a flight with another airline as she had to get home for one of their daughters' medical procedure. The remaining three of us had to stay over another night and fly out the next day.

On the flight home, Paul reiterated to me a statement he had made on the top of a Swiss mountain: "I am going to find God." When Paul Henderson makes a commitment to something, look out. A good example is the day he challenged himself to win the open golf championship at the Mississauga

Golf and Country Club. In short order, he accomplished the feat after his sixtieth birthday, defeating much younger competitors, many of whom were scratch golfers.

Paul was relentless on his journey and drove people crazy – among them Mel Stevens from Teen Ranch – trying to get answers to his questions. I believe that in the end, as Paul made himself open to Christian principles, God found him, and shortly afterwards Nora invited the Lord into her life. Paul challenged Jan and me to consider our spiritual life, and with the help of godly friends such as Mel Stevens and their prayers, we also became believers.

As professional athletes, we tend to concentrate on developing ourselves physically, intellectually, and emotionally, often neglecting the spiritual side of life. Thanks to someone who cared about me, I finally addressed the issue of what I knew was missing in my life and now feel totally complete in the Lord.

After a storied hockey career, Paul considered the financial investment industry as a possible new opportunity. During our playing days together, he had been very much into the stock market. It was obvious to all around him at the time that he would be very successful in this field of endeavour. But the Lord had a different plan, and after much prayer and discussion with advisers, Paul joined a ministry that would in time find him affecting the spiritual lives of countless executives across our country. I have met many of the men whose lives have been changed through Paul's ministry. As Rick Warren says in his book *The Purpose-Driven Life,* these men, myself included, have found that being successful and fulfilling your life's purpose are not at all the same issue.

Thank you, my friend, for being my linemate and my brother in the Lord. I am truly grateful for the journey we have travelled together following that life-changing event on March 3, 1968.

Ron Ellis
Toronto, Ontario
January 10, 2012

INTRODUCTION PAUL HENDERSON

WHAT IS THE GOAL OF YOUR LIFE?

That's a question nobody ever asks me because they all think they know the answer when it comes to Paul Henderson. They all just assume that the "goal" of my life was the one I scored on September 28, 1972.

I slid a puck past Vladislav Tretiak that day to give Canada the Summit Series win over the Russians in Moscow, and that goal certainly changed my life forever. No doubt it was the biggest goal I ever scored in a hockey game, and because of it, a lot more people know who Paul Henderson is than would have if I hadn't scored it. It's been called the Goal of the Century, after all, and being the player who scored it certainly gives me some instant recognition in our wonderful and hockey-mad country.

Before that epic series in 1972, you had to be a fairly dedicated hockey fan to know the name Paul Henderson. I had a good, solid career, don't get me wrong, but that goal gave me a stature in this country that would not have been possible unless I'd converted that rebound in game eight.

It certainly was the goal of my life on the ice. When something you did is recognized as the Canadian sports moment of the century, well, it's very satisfying. When that happens, you can do two things – run away and hide from it or embrace it. I made a conscious decision to embrace it, and I have done just that all of my life. So yes, The Goal certainly was the goal of my life from that standpoint.

And I will talk about it later on in this book, as I have talked about it for many years. I never get tired of hearing somebody's story of where they were when the goal was scored and what the goal meant to them, or being asked yet again what happened leading up to it. I love talking about all aspects of it. Like I said, I embrace it.

But if you ask me the question, "What is the goal of your life?" then you might be surprised to hear my answer. That goal was my on-ice highlight, without question – how can it not be? – but I read that question differently. The goal of a person's life has nothing to do with the kind of goals a hockey player scores on the ice; the goal of a person's life is their purpose, their personal answer as to why they are on this planet and what they want to do with their life.

It took me a long time to answer that question for myself, and a lot of soul-searching. But the goal of my life has nothing to do with any hockey game.

INTRODUCTION ROGER LAJOIE

JUST LIKE EVERYBODY ELSE WHO IS OLD ENOUGH TO remember Thursday, September 28, 1972, I have a Paul Henderson story about where I was when The Goal was scored.

I was fourteen years old, in grade eight at LaSalle Catholic Comprehensive High School. Unlike some other students, I didn't take the day off school to watch the game, even though I was a huge hockey fan (still am to this day, of course). I didn't have to because there were television sets at school so students could watch, as there had been all week.

Because of the time difference, it was the middle of the school day while the games from Russia were on, and the ever-wise teachers at our school decided that if students knew the game was on TV at school, maybe they'd actually go to school instead of skipping class. That fact – and the fact that my mother would definitely not have approved of skipping class to watch a hockey game – ensured I was at school when game eight from Moscow was on.

Even though there were televisions all over the school, if I remember correctly, the prime viewing locations for the game were in the gym or in the library.

We had a teacher at the school named Edna Gardner who was a stern disciplinarian. You did not fool around with Mrs. Gardner, but even she realized that the magnitude of this hockey game took precedence over the run-of-the-mill day at school in late September.

She was stationed in the library, where there had to be hundreds of kids gathered around the TV taking in the final minutes of the game. Clearly she did not approve of such a mass of students in one area, and normally she was so stern that she'd just stare any student down who dared not to be in class at any given moment in the day (I was scared to death of her, I freely admit that now). But even she laid low, just surveying us all with her steely eagle eyes while we watched the final minutes unfold.

When that Paul Henderson shot slid past Vladislav Tretiak, the library, normally a sanctuary of silence, exploded into a crescendo of noise that only several hundred students delirious with joy could have possibly made. I mean, so help me God, the walls in that room shook from the eruption of sound.

I remember the delirious cheers, I can even remember Foster Hewitt's infamous "Henderson has scored for Canada!" call. But I can also remember Edna Gardner's screams too, as she demanded that we all calm down as she snapped off the TV set in an attempt to quell what I'm sure she thought was going to be a riot.

She needn't have worried. There was no anger in that response, just pure joy mixed in with a palatable sense of relief. We all believed that there was no way Canada was going to lose that Summit Series to the Russians, and by God, we didn't. Thanks to Paul Henderson, of course.

So fast-forward nearly forty years later, and my friends at Heritage Hockey ask me to help to put together the story of Paul Henderson in time for the fortieth anniversary of the Goal of the Century. We'll call it *The Goal of My Life*, they tell me, which is a sort of double entendre of The Goal in Russia and Paul's ultimate goal of the purpose statement that he follows in his life.

To many Canadians under the age of forty, Paul Henderson is as much known for being a Christian as he is a hockey player. To those of us on the north side of forty, he'll always be better known as the player who scored the biggest goal in the history of hockey in this country (and sorry, Darryl Sittler, Mario Lemieux, and Sidney Crosby, his goal was bigger. Trust me, you had to be there to understand. There is really no argument – if you were alive in 1972, you know why).

So my task was simple: meet with Paul Henderson as often as possible, listen to his stories, and write eighty thousand words in his voice. And the end result of that is what you hold in your hands today.

This was my pleasure, believe me. In many ways it was my honour, without trying to sound too sappy about it. Paul Henderson's final story to the world, in his words, all about The Goal of His Life – I was just thrilled to do it.

Paul has lived a dynamic and fascinating life both on and off the ice. He beat the odds just by making it to the NHL out of Lucknow, Ontario, and enjoyed a solid professional hockey career. He scored the most important goal in Canadian hockey history, but he battled demons after that for several years. He finally found his calling to his ministry, but only after being denied careers as a broker and as a broadcaster. It was an interesting road he travelled.

Paul Henderson's life story can teach us a lot of things about perseverance and discovering what really matters in life. But it taught me – or I guess I should be honest and say it reminded me, as I've always really known this – that no good or bad things happen to us: everything is indifferent. It's our attitude and how we react to life's challenges that make an experience good or bad for us.

Paul had a challenging relationship with his father, for instance, which can be bad; but without it, he knows he wouldn't have become the player that he became. His father was clearly a driving force in his life, but he was also a demanding man, as you'll read later, and could be very hard on Paul. As Paul says many years later, he spent a lot of his life, especially his younger life, trying to please his father.

Paul Henderson scored the biggest goal in Canadian hockey history, which can be great; but that fame led to perhaps the darkest period of his life. He was denied careers as a broker and broadcaster, which can be bad; but those roadblocks led him to his true calling and a satisfaction that he could never have achieved without that adversity.

What a story it is, and what a challenge this will be, I thought as I sat down to help him put it all together. Now, where to start? Well, as the ever-wise Dorothy said in *The Wizard of Oz*, the best place to start . . . is at the beginning.

CHAPTER ONE

IT IS WISE TO FOLLOW YOUR PASSION IN LIFE. IF YOU aren't passionate about something, there is little chance you can be excited about it and enjoy what you do.

As a young man, I had a passion for sports, and for hockey in particular, so I chose to follow my passion. From the time I started playing, I dreamed about being an NHL player, right from the very start. I loved the game of hockey and I was good at it. You get confidence when you are good at something, and I was good at hockey. But like anyone who is fortunate enough to make it to the National Hockey League, the road for me wasn't a direct one by any means.

I was born on January 28, 1943, in Kincardine, Ontario, on the eastern shore of Lake Huron. My dad, Garnet, had gone overseas with the Canadian Army the previous September, and my mother, Evelyn, was visiting his parents at their farm in Amberley. She went into labour at the worst possible time, just as a massive snowstorm hit, blocking all the roads. The nearest hospital was in Kincardine, ten miles away. It was left to my grandfather, William Henderson, to hitch up the horses to a sleigh, venture out onto the frozen surface of Lake Huron, and try to make it there, in freezing-cold temperatures. Mom gave birth to me on the sleigh before we made it to the hospital, and by the time they finally arrived, I had started to turn blue. Quite the first day of my life, to be sure, but I made it.

When I was three, my father came back after the war and returned to his job as a station agent for the Canadian National Railway. He worked for them in Kincardine, Exeter, and Port Colborne, before we finally settled in Lucknow, just north of Goderich.

Garnet Henderson was an imposing man who was over six feet tall, weighed more than 280 pounds, and had a quick temper. You didn't want to mess around with him – although he never hit me or my brother or sisters, I was petrified of the man. He could pick up two ninety-pound milk cans in one hand when he was just fifteen years old, and later on, while he was working during the winter at the CN station in Lucknow, he single-handedly lifted a car that had skidded off the station's platform onto the tracks. Was he strong? He also once hoisted a six-hundred-pound barrel of salt off the floor and onto a scale just on a dare, if you want strong!

But although I wasn't as strong as my dad or didn't have his temper, I did inherit some things from him, including his drive and determination, along with some natural athletic ability.

Dad was an okay athlete, certainly not a star who played several sports, but he was exceptionally fast on his feet. But there was no way he was going to develop any kind of a career since he grew up on a farm, got married at an early age in 1941, and then went off to the Second World War. When he returned, he had a young family to look after.

Dad really enjoyed coaching baseball and hockey. Although he might not have been the greatest strategist as a coach, he would do anything for the kids who played for him. He was always there to help them out in any way possible, and all his players really appreciated his commitment to coaching and to them as people.

Dad was a big-hearted man, and at the railway station he would often give people their COD packages even when they didn't have the money to pay. They'd promise to pay later, but he'd often wind up having to cover it himself. There is no doubt in my mind that his compassionate side taught me to be understanding of the needs of other people too.

Like many men of his era, I guess, Dad was tough to talk to on a serious level. He was guarded, and I was afraid of him, so we never did develop a real closeness like I have with my kids today.

While in Germany during the war, he barely survived a mortar shelling that killed eight other men. His jaw was smashed, but a surgeon did a marvellous job of reconstruction. That wound healed, but the memory of it remained buried inside him, as he just wouldn't talk about his war experiences.

He had his limitations as a coach, and his temper often got in the way, especially when dealing with young kids. But I never doubted that he was really proud of me and the player I was becoming. I would need better coaching down the line for sure – I was basically getting by on raw ability as a kid – but he helped me a lot, especially in building my confidence. I have him to thank for my career in the NHL.

I think he wanted me to make the NHL as much as I wanted to make it.

I was nine years old before I got my first pair of skates, and they were used ones – we couldn't afford new. I took to skating quickly. I always had great speed on and off skates, and that certainly was a major asset to me in the game, especially when I got into pro hockey.

Mom was always worried about injuries, as many moms would be. But she supported me and did what she could do to help me along the way, always being the encouraging one. My mom and I were very close, so similar in personality, and we were a fairly close-knit family. My parents tried to do what was best for me, my brother Bruce, and my sisters Marilyn, Carolyn, and Sandra. We didn't have a lot of money, but our parents did provide a good home for all of us.

Dad suffered a serious stroke at the age of forty-two, which I think was mainly due to stress and a terrible diet. He never recovered from it fully; the doctors told us he had likely experienced one or two minor heart attacks prior to the stroke but had just fought them off and kept going. He was only given a year to live after the stroke, but he fooled them all until dying at the age of forty-nine in 1968.

It's funny how much my relationship with my father affected so much of my life and the person that I am today, albeit in many an inadvertent way. In taking another long look back at my life, I can see where much of my confidence comes from. It came from my dad, which is amazing to me in some ways. Ironically, what I thought was one of the worst things my dad ever did to me might have resulted in me having the kind of confidence I've had all my life.

My dad was always demanding of me, and was seldom

complimentary toward me, no matter what I did. He was a product of his times, an old-school, chauvinistic man who didn't understand psychology or how to handle children. He coached me a lot growing up, and I'd score three, four, or even five goals in a game and he would still get on me. He'd always be nitpicking about something I hadn't done instead of praising me for what I did. It was just the way he was, but I knew that he was very proud of me – because he'd be coaching me and he wouldn't let me off the ice! I'd be on a forward line and he'd make me stay out there and play defence to catch my breath instead of taking me off. He wanted me out on the ice all the time.

I remember one time when he was coaching me in peewee and we were losing the game and he was angry. He walked into the dressing room during an intermission and said, "Listen up, you guys. Just give the puck to Paul and get the hell out of his way." I thought it was just a terrible thing to say to the other players, who were all my friends. I couldn't even look up and face them. How humiliating that was for me then, how embarrassing, having my father basically tell the rest of my team that they weren't good enough but I was. After that game, however, I also remember thinking that my dad thought I was good – really good – and I felt so pleased that he was that proud of me.

I never forgot that moment and still think about it to this day. At the time, I was so embarrassed by what he said. I didn't like him treating my friends that way and putting me on the spot. But as I grew older and more mature, it dawned on me that my father had affirmed me, and he was very proud of me. I have since read that every young man needs to be affirmed by his father to really become a man. I agree.

I was a confident kid and dreamed that I could turn out to be a hockey player. I was so confident that I started practising my autograph when I was in grade five for when I made it to the NHL! Where did that come from? Today, I believe that much of it came from that incident when my father affirmed me in front of my teammates.

My dad and I had our issues, but he was the person who convinced me that I wouldn't be able to live with myself if I didn't give hockey a real shot when I wanted to quit the game in junior, and his perhaps misguided affirmation of me as a young man gave me the self-confidence I needed to get to that level to start with.

So given all this, what are the odds of a kid from Lucknow, Ontario, making it all the way to the NHL? Pretty high, I imagine.

Sports were a big part of my life at an early age, and I was a good athlete just like my parents were. Both of them were very quick and strong runners, so the genes were good for me. I played football and baseball (I was on a championship baseball team when I was sixteen years old), but hockey really turned out to be my thing, and my greatest asset as I developed was my speed.

I was also a pretty good student most of the time, especially when I was motivated to learn something. In grade six I got really serious about academics, as my competitive side came out in the classroom. There were two girls in our class who were excellent students and always had the highest marks. After seeing their report cards one term, I just decided then and there that I was going to be the one with the highest marks by the time the next report card came around. I put my mind to it, and sure enough, I was able to do it.

I credit playing team sports for teaching me great life lessons. When you are successful in a team sport, it instills confidence and a sense of belonging, of being part of something bigger than yourself. You always feel better when you know you have done your very best for yourself and your team. You learn that there are no shortcuts to success, and that hard work pays off in the long run. You realize that you need others to do well for you to succeed, and that the more you try to be a good team player, the better things will go for you individually. When you win as a team and start excelling, you get great satisfaction from that winning, and that becomes addictive.

But despite all that, my fear of being poor nearly did indeed stop me from pursuing a pro hockey career, and it took my dad to convince me not to give up on the game too early.

There really is no other way to say it than this: we were poor. We didn't have much money for anything, and our family had a lot of debt. It was a real problem in our household. My parents didn't understand what a lot of people don't, especially today. You have to spend less money than you make – that's the simple truth that so many people just can't seem to come to grips with. My dad got sucked into that debt trap, and it made it very hard on all of us while I was growing up. The arguments and fights my parents had were almost always because of a lack of money.

You learn how to look after yourself when you are in a situation like that when you are young. I vowed that I would never live like that when I got older; I wouldn't let a lack of money become an issue for me the way it was for my parents.

By the time I was in grade nine I was basically self-sufficient in terms of making money on my own. I always found jobs to make money, from piling wood, to picking apples, to working on a farm. I worked at Cyril Brown's grocery store from 4:00 p.m. until 6:30 p.m. every weekday and every Saturday from 9:00 a.m. until 11:00 p.m. Working all those hours allowed me to have enough money to clothe myself and to get some of the things I wanted. My parents sure couldn't afford to give me most of those things.

As a result, I have always understood the value of money and living within your means. I paid cash for almost everything, and although I had a mortgage on the first house I ever bought, since then I've paid for everything in cash. I've always lived with the dread of going into debt.

That job in the grocery store not only helped me with my financial situation, it also helped me to find the woman who would turn out to be my wife for five decades, the great love of my life. I knew very quickly that Eleanor Alton was the one for me, right from the time I first saw her in the summer of 1959. The absolute best decision I ever made was the one I made regarding the woman I chose as my life's partner. I don't know anybody who lives life better as wife, mother, and grandmother than Eleanor does. She is definitely my rock and the love of my life.

The thing that made it so easy for me to decide that she was the one was that I had already decided on what I was looking for in a wife. I believe that you won't find what you're looking for until you know what it is you're looking for. I wasn't after a career-minded woman; I was looking for someone who wanted to be a wife and a mother more than having a career. Sure, looks are always important to a young guy, but more than that I wanted someone with common sense, someone who was willing to work, and someone who definitely was not a prima donna or in any way a drama queen.

I was a product of my generation, I guess, and I felt I was to be the provider and she'd be the stay-at-home mom to our children. And she had to be a really great cook! My mom, whom I loved dearly, was an okay cook, but I learned from my aunts the difference between being an okay cook and a great cook. And for sure I wanted a great cook for a wife!

Eleanor filled the bill in every way and more. What a sensational wife and partner to me she has been every step of the way.

Within a month after our first date, I told her she was the girl I was set on to marry.

"I'm going to marry you, Eleanor; you can forget about everyone else," I told her straight out.

"Well, aren't you arrogant," was her straight-to-the-point reply.

Needless to say, it took her a little longer to embrace the idea that we were made for each other! But I'd say within the first year she came to the same conclusion that I had already come to – and thank God she did.

I first laid eyes on her at Cyril Brown's fruit market in Lucknow. In she came, with a friend, and I immediately went to work to try to impress this slim fifteen-year-old girl with beautiful brown hair while the two were looking at some lettuce.

"Can I help you?" I asked.

"We're looking for some lettuce," Eleanor replied.

"Don't touch that stuff," I said, immediately showing my expertise. "Wait right here. I will take care of you."

I walked quickly to the back of the store and got some really fresh lettuce. I had to go through several boxes until I found two huge heads that were just perfect. I cleaned them off, slicked back my Brylcreemed hair in Elvis Presley style, and returned acting as cool as – well, a head of lettuce, I guess!

I wasn't nearly as suave as I thought I was, but I did manage to converse with Eleanor long enough to get that all-important phone number.

From the moment we started dating, I loved everything about her. I liked to dance, and she was such a terrific dancer and could follow me anywhere on the dance floor. She looked so great out there and I was so proud to be seen with her.

She was a worker too, let's make no mistake about that. I remember for our first date, I came to get her when she was working on her parents' farm. While I waited for her to finish milking the cows, I asked her how I could help. She told me it'd be a big help if I could assist her in carrying the milk to the separators in the same containers she was already carrying.

I was happy to help – until I picked one up and realized how heavy they were! She, however, managed to lift them with relative ease, and she looked just great doing it. Holy mackerel, I thought to myself, is this girl ever strong! It was obvious to me that she knew how to work and that she had to be responsible to do the milking on her own while her father and brothers were working in the fields.

She cleaned up and we drove off to Goderich for our first date. It was a Friday night and I was feeling like a million bucks, sitting next to the prettiest girl in the world.

It was then time to show her just how suave this Paul Henderson guy was and buy her something to eat. We went to Pete's Hot Dog Stand.

I got out of the car and ordered two foot-long hot dogs, two large orders of fries, and two giant Cokes. I was all set to hand Eleanor her hot dog, fries, and Coke – but the tray slipped from my hand and fell into her lap, and the Coke, relish, and ketchup destroyed her white linen skirt. Disaster! I just wanted to crawl under that car and let it run over me, I was so embarrassed! It was terrible. But fortunately for me, Eleanor had a great sense of humour – enough of one to agree to see this joker again, despite that mess!

We started dating when I was sixteen and she was fifteen, and we got married very young, when I was nineteen and she was eighteen, on November 10, 1962. We'll celebrate fifty years together in 2012, God willing, so I really made the right call on this one.

I made a vow to her right from the start of our relationship.

"We'll never be poor," I said to her. "I don't care what it takes: I'm going to be successful. I don't want to live like my parents."

I took that vow very seriously, and even though I was sure I had the talent to be an NHL player, I also knew that getting a good education was critical for me – what would happen if I couldn't make the grade and make a living playing in the NHL?

My junior hockey career was winding down. We'd won the Memorial Cup in 1962, and I had just one more year of junior eligibility left. Eleanor and I talked about our future, and we both felt that giving up hockey and getting an education was the way to go for me. I had pretty much decided that I would give up on the game and get a university education – an education that would provide a good future and foundation for Eleanor and myself – and I wouldn't be in the same position my parents had been in for so many years.

Eleanor was then and still is today my biggest backer and supporter. She was with me in whatever decision I made, but there was still the matter of telling this to my dad, who had spent so much time coaching me over the years.

I have to admit I dreaded having to tell my father the news. Up until that time, I had had only peripheral conversations with him, as we really didn't know how to communicate with each other. He was a product of his times – he ran the household and would seldom discuss things even with my mother – so I was really hesitant to tell him my plans.

I knew I had to, however, so I sat my dad down and told him what I had in mind, and I thought he'd go crazy.

He shocked me. He didn't get angry at all. In fact, he sat and listened to what I had to say, and maybe for the first time in our lives, we had a really meaningful conversation about my future and what I should be doing with my life.

Not only didn't he yell and get mad and call me a fool, but he also didn't tell me to change my mind – at least not immediately. His advice hit right to the point.

"Think about this," he told me. "The one thing that I think will drive you crazy is that on a Saturday night when you're watching *Hockey Night in Canada,* you'll be asking yourself, 'Could I have made it?' Think about that. I think it will drive you crazy not knowing if you could have made it. I really believe you can make it and I think that you really believe that also."

It was great advice, and important advice for me to consider at that time. I thought it over and talked to Eleanor about it and we decided that I would play my last year of junior, really give it my best shot, and if I didn't make it to the NHL in the next two years, then I could quit the game and move on and get my education. Then and only then could I watch *Hockey Night in Canada* and not wonder, "What if?"

I had to really find out if I was good enough. And the only way to do that was to do everything I could to make a career out of hockey. Well, I did just that, and I led the league in scoring, I was a first team all-star right-winger, and I was considered an NHL prospect. I made it to Detroit the next year, and it went on from there.

That decision, of course, opened up a world of possibilities for me and for my family. NHL salaries then weren't like they are now, but hockey was a good career and there was a good life possible after it too, with many opportunities available for former players that weren't available for people who had never played the game.

Hockey allowed me and my family to enjoy a very good life, one very different from the one my parents had. And it was my father's convincing me to give it a real shot that led me to get over my fear of being poor and freed me to do what it took to play in the NHL. I have him to thank for all that.

Oddly enough, my hockey career started in the basement of a Chinese restaurant, and with balls, not with pucks.

Charlie Chin, a Chinese immigrant, opened a restaurant in Lucknow in the 1940s, and I would head there to play ball hockey in the basement of the restaurant with five of his sons, who were all pretty good players but far too small to play the game at the professional level. But they were good enough to draw large crowds to the Lucknow Arena to watch them play, and it was the start to my own playing days.

I'd played a lot of pond hockey, of course, like all kids did back in those days. Two friends of mine in particular, Murray and Bob Hunter, would spend hours on end with me playing hockey on a pond near their home. That's where you really develop a true love for the game, playing with your friends.

I had a fair amount of natural athletic ability, to be sure, and great speed, and later on I developed a very good shot from playing all that fun hockey with my buddies. By the time I got to peewee, I was a frequent goal scorer, and I demonstrated that for the first time at a tournament in Goderich.

That peewee tournament had teams from as far away as Winnipeg, and I scored six goals in one of the games. That led to the first daily newspaper article with my name in it, which was a really great thrill for me. After that, teams basically double-teamed me to try to slow me down, which my always competitive father/coach didn't like in the least! But it was an early sign that maybe I did have some special talents as a player.

We were from a small town, but that didn't hurt my cause at all. There weren't enough players to go around for a lot of teams because of the size of the place, so I got to play bantam, midget, and juvenile hockey all in the same season. That also meant I was often times playing against players as much as four years older than I was – but that really only made me better in the long run.

When I was fifteen I had the greatest game of my life up until that point – and I guess when you consider that I scored eighteen goals in one game, it has to stand as my greatest individual game ever! That performance came in a juvenile playoff game between Lucknow and Wainfleet, a 21–6 win, and I also had two assists – just to show that I was the complete package, ha ha!

My dad had always told me to take my first shot at the goalie's head, just to unnerve him, so I always fired a high, hard one right away. In that game everything went in – I had four goals on my first shift! – and for the first time I attracted the attention of some scouts. By the way, in case you want to know, the secret to scoring eighteen goals in one game is to find a very bad goalie to play against!

My eighteen-goal game got a nice article in the *London Free Press*, and after hearing about my performance, some professional scouts took notice. The first major step in my career – playing at the major junior level – was about to take place.

CHAPTER TWO

THREE NHL TEAMS – HALF OF THE LEAGUE AT THE time – expressed interest in signing me. Those teams were Toronto, Boston, and Detroit. Boston's scout, Baldy Cotton, came to our house to speak with my dad. They were not a strong team then, from my father's perspective (he was a big Red Wings fan!), but because of that he thought I might have a better chance to make the NHL if I went with them and they wanted me, so I decided to attend their junior team's training camp the following year in Niagara Falls.

When Jimmy Skinner, the Detroit scout, heard about my plans, he suggested I skate with their junior team in Hamilton for a few days to help me prepare for Niagara Falls. I figured why not, since I hadn't signed anything at that point, and the Hamilton camp started three days prior to the one in Niagara Falls. After the three days there, Skinner told me that the Red Wings would sign me if I would agree to the terms with them, and that way I wouldn't have to worry about going to the Bruins camp in Niagara Falls and perhaps getting cut. Hamilton was also closer to my home, and after talking it over with Eleanor, I decided to sign with the Red Wings. Boston wasn't the least bit happy with Detroit; they felt I had a future with them and that the Red Wings had stolen me from them. But the decision was made: I was going to sign with the Red Wings.

I needed plenty of playing time, that was the most important thing, and a chance to display and practise my skills. When they asked me to consider playing with the Goderich Sailors, their junior B team (which was close to Lucknow), I readily agreed. Goderich was just forty kilometres from Lucknow, and I could continue going to school and also be closer to Eleanor. That was a perfect fit for me. At sixteen, I was their youngest player. I enjoyed a good year there playing on a line with Carlo Rossi and Darcy Oliver.

The next season, 1960–61, I was back in Hamilton but didn't play a regular shift. I killed penalties and saw spot duty because my coach, Eddie Bush, knew I still wasn't ready for junior A. They decided to send me down to the junior B Hamilton Bees, where I scored eighteen goals in twelve games, after which I finished the season with the junior A team for their playoffs.

Things really took off for me in 1961–62 when Hamilton won the Memorial Cup. I played a lot, had twenty-four goals in fifty games, and was part of a great ride to the toughest trophy championship to win in hockey, the Memorial Cup. What a terrific season that was for me and the team.

We beat the St. Catharines Teepees, who had Phil Esposito, Dennis Hull, and Ken Hodge in their lineup, in six games. It also took us six games to eliminate the Niagara Falls Flyers, with J.P. Parise and Terry Crisp, while St. Michael's, featuring Rod Seiling, took us five games to conquer. We also eliminated the Quebec Citadelles in four games.

In the final against Edmonton, I scored a goal in the last game (played in Kitchener; the series was played in Guelph and Hamilton as well, so all the games weren't home games for us), and we won the championship that night. It's still a wonderful memory after all these years. We had great players like Pit Martin (thirty-six goals), Lowell MacDonald (forty-eight goals to lead the Ontario Hockey Association), and my centreman and our captain, Howie Menard.

Eddie Bush, an old-school coach, was great for my development as a player that season. He was strict and headstrong, but he taught me the importance of defensive hockey. I worked on that aspect of my game, to the point where I later became known as a solid defensive player and a good team guy. Bush also insisted that his players be clean-cut – he hated long hair on his players – and made me get a brush cut. We also had to wear a jacket and tie everywhere. Ever since then, I've paid attention to maintaining a professional-looking appearance.

What a special season that was, and what a thrill to be able to win the Memorial Cup. MacDonald and Martin were just magic together, two of the top forwards in all of junior hockey at that time. They really provided the bulk of the scoring and were terrific together playing on a line with Joe Bagosa on the wing.

Pit was such a star in junior hockey; he was smart on the ice and he could really do it all. He was such a great playmaker, and there were no weaknesses in his game. He was a go-to guy on offence, and that line really clicked.

I played on a line that season with Menard, who was a tremendous centre, and a left-winger by the name of John Grafton, another pretty good junior player. Menard was such a fireball, he really inspired us, and he was a good leader in the dressing room. We were the grinding line, but with my speed I could sometimes create some chances, so we were a solid unit. I always took pride in my defensive game, and we played an important role on a team that won a championship, which was very satisfying.

We had a terrific defence as well, led by Bobby Wall, one of the best defenceman in all of junior A hockey, and we were a tough team to play against, thanks primarily to a guy by the name of Ronnie Harris.

Harris was by far the toughest guy in the league, and did he ever make us play braver. Especially in junior hockey, it was really good to know we had the toughest guy in the world sitting right there on the bench. And just like a lot of tough guys – guys like John Ferguson, for example – he was one of the nicest people in the world off the ice. But put a pair of skates on him, and he would get that glaze in his eyes. It's kind of like Jekyll and Hyde – guys like that become crazy! The toughness Ronnie added to our team made him really valuable.

Our goalie, Buddy Bloom, was outstanding that year as well. He was my roommate, a great guy, and we never would have won the Memorial Cup without him. He was just incredible in the playoffs and was so dedicated to hockey.

Honestly, Buddy was the straightest guy you'd ever want to meet. He never dated while in junior hockey, and never took so much as one drink. He was all about school and hockey with us, and he later went on to the University of Denver instead of staying and trying to play in the minor pros.

Funny thing: once he got to Denver, he went from being the straightest guy in the world to the wildest! He really let loose once he got away from junior hockey. But Buddy was just tremendous for us, and like I said, we couldn't have won without him.

As great as that season was, the summer after the Memorial Cup win was a difficult one for me. That was the time I started wondering whether the life of a hockey player was for me. As I said, I had the dread of being poor and was considering getting on with my university education – until my dad convinced me to give it one more shot and make it a real shot.

Eddie Bush was also very helpful to me then.

"You have the skating ability, the strength, and the desire to play in the NHL," he said. "You work hard, and that hard work will pay off for you. Let others play tough and get into fights. You go out and score goals. Play aggressively, but don't fight. Use your speed and shot to get goals. Fighters are a dime a dozen. Goal scoring will get you into the NHL."

Bush was right. Along with my dad, he really made me stay focused on hockey and told me exactly what I needed to do to make it to the next level.

In my final season of junior hockey, 1962–63, I really blossomed. I scored forty-nine goals in forty-eight games to lead the OHA. Even though we didn't have nearly as good a team as we did in winning the Memorial Cup – we had a very young team, as many of our players had turned pro after the Cup win or were just too old to play junior A anymore – I had a good year. Buddy Bloom was a huge help to me. We'd stay after practice and he'd let me fire snap shots at him until we were both exhausted, so I developed a really quick release. Everybody fires the puck quickly these days, of course, but back then I was known for snapping the puck quickly, and Buddy really helped me work on that shot. Pit Martin was second to me in goals with thirty-six that year, so I was really on my way to a career in the NHL.

I loved my time in junior hockey – what kid from a small town wouldn't? The travel was pretty easy, as there were only eight teams in the league and most of the bus trips were short. The Montreal Junior Canadiens were in the league and were our farthest rival. We took the train to play them, and that was a pretty big deal to us, but most of the time it was off to St. Catharines, Guelph, Peterborough, Niagara Falls, and Toronto. We had our fun, but we took the game seriously too, so all in all it was a great time, and it helped me develop into a more mature person and a better hockey player.

I have to admit I was pretty green! I remember one night during my first year in Hamilton we got to go to a steak house in town before going to play in Peterborough, but I wasn't really looking forward to it because I didn't like steak – the only steak I'd had was at home, and my mother used to overcook it in the frying pan! And this place was pretty nice too – the kind of restaurant I'd never been to before.

We got there, and I saw that there were two forks at each place setting. I thought, What the heck? Two forks – what's that for? I didn't have a clue that one was for salad, of course! Then they asked us what kind of dressing we wanted on our salad – first time I was ever asked that! The guy next to me said, "French," so guess what I ordered – French! I had no idea what that was all about. And when they asked how we wanted our steak cooked, I was just as lost! The guy next to me said, "Medium," so I got mine medium too, whatever that was. I was amazed to discover that I loved steak that wasn't well done!

But playing in Hamilton was a tremendous experience for me in a lot of ways. The Red Wings were monitoring my progress, and there was no doubt that they considered me a bona fide prospect. I was getting a lot of attention in the local Hamilton media, and I felt I might get a chance at some point to show them what I could do at the NHL level. But I never thought that chance would come as quickly as it did.

In early April 1963, I got an unexpected call-up from Detroit. Floyd Smith was injured and Bruce MacGregor's father had died, and they needed a right-winger for the last two games of the regular season, so it was time for me to make my NHL debut. I was instructed to report to Toronto for the first game in a weekend home-and-home series with the Maple Leafs. I was excited, naturally, but I think my father was even more so. He drove to Hamilton and picked me up, and then drove me to the game. For an hour in the car, he hammered away at me, telling me I had to make a good first impression. He told me I should go out there and nail the first guy I had a chance to hit.

"Get out there, son, and show them you are a player. Get out there and nail someone!" Those were his words of advice to me. He was so proud of the fact that his son was going to play an NHL game and that he would get to see it.

I didn't get into the game until the second period. When I finally got my first shift, I darted off the bench and onto the ice, determined to make a huge impression, with my dad's words still ringing in my ears.

So what did I do? I elbowed Dick Duff in the head eight seconds into my first shift! Off came Duff's gloves and I was in my first NHL fight. We threw a few punches and I managed to wrestle him to the ice. I could have really drilled him, as I had him in a headlock, but I wasn't a fighter and neither was he. So the referee stepped in and pulled us apart before either one of us did something stupid.

Eight seconds into my NHL career and there I was, sitting in the penalty box for seven minutes – two for elbowing and five for fighting. While I was in there, two veteran Leafs players, Eddie Shack and Bobby Baun, skated by, calling me every name in the book and telling me they'd be coming after me the first chance they got. I'm sure my new teammates were wondering just who the heck this Henderson guy was! What a way to make your first impression in the NHL.

I was saved that night, however, when Toronto took a penalty while I was in the box; the second my penalty ended, coach Sid Abel motioned me back to the bench to get our power-play unit on the ice. I leaped back over the boards onto the safety of that bench with just as much enthusiasm as I did coming onto the ice for my first NHL shift. That was the extent of Paul Henderson's first contribution to the NHL.

The next night we were back in Detroit against the Leafs, and my father wasn't there – thank goodness! – for my first game in the Olympia. That was another historic building and another thrill, to play a home game in that great old barn. This time, I managed to get on the ice in the first period, although well into it. This time, my "victim" was Frank Mahovlich. Abel told me my job was to check Mahovlich and not let him get away from me, which was not an easy assignment. I lasted all of maybe ten seconds as Mahovlich got past me quickly on the outside, so I whacked him with a two-hander and down he went. He bounced right back up and came after me enraged, but before I could get into my second NHL fight, the linesman stepped in and saved me – to my relief, as I had no desire to fight a very angry Frank Mahovlich. The referee gave me a two-minute penalty for slashing.

Boy, now the Leafs were really ready to kill me! But as soon as the penalty expired, an offside was called and once again Abel called me back to the bench.

"For God's sake, Henderson, can't you stay on the ice?" Abel hollered at me. I didn't see the ice again, so my big weekend NHL debut saw me play maybe twenty seconds and take nine minutes in penalties in two games. How is that for making an impact?

I wanted to play in the NHL very badly, but after that experience and the following year during my first NHL camp, I realized I had a lot of things to work on before I would be ready for full-time duty. There was a huge difference between junior A and the NHL, but at least I had gotten a taste of what it was like.

During my first NHL training camp with the Detroit Red Wings in September 1963, it was clear to me I still didn't have enough experience to play in the NHL. It was only in my last two seasons of junior A that I had really gotten the chance to play a lot. To make the leap to the NHL was really more than I could handle at that time. Detroit had a lot of young and upcoming players at that camp – guys like Pit Martin, Larry Jeffrey, Lowell MacDonald, and Bob Wall. Even though I had a good camp and was probably the fastest skater there, I was sent down to Pittsburgh. I actually asked them if I could go to the American Hockey League, if you can believe that. They also felt it would be beneficial for me, as I had a lot of things I needed to work on and I was still very young. I needed to get some real playing time with the pros, and it was where I felt – and the Red Wings felt – I should be. I had to get stronger and play smarter to earn my way onto a full-time roster in the NHL.

The American Hockey League was a terrific place to learn and play the game. I can't say enough about my time there. The AHL was a very competitive league. In a six-team NHL, there were only jobs for about sixty-five forwards, so you know there were a lot of really good players in the AHL. Some of them were career minor leaguers, some of them were just a step away from the NHL, and the competition for jobs and high quality of play really helped me develop into a better player.

We had a good team in Pittsburgh, and a mostly older one – Pit Martin and I were the only young guys. Vic Stasiuk, who had played with Chicago, Boston, and Detroit for many years and been a member of the Bruins' famous Uke Line with Jerry Toppazini and Bronco Horvath, was the playing coach, and he played me a lot, in all situations, which really helped me to improve. My linemates certainly helped me also. Winger Yves Locas led the AHL that year with forty goals and my centre, Art Stratton, had a league-best sixty-five assists.

The players were great, and they were a tight-knit group. Many of them knew they would never play in the NHL, so they just enjoyed their time in a league with long bus drives and long hours socializing after the game.

Veteran players like Hank Ciesla, Pete Geogan, Lou Marcon, Adam Keller, Claude Laforge, Yves Locas, and Art Stratton were such a great help to a young aspiring – but very green – kid like myself. We'd kill time on the road-trip bus listening to players like our wily defenceman, Warren Godfrey, who always had a great story to tell.

The league was full of characters like Godfrey and also full of hard-nosed guys like Don Cherry and Fred Glover. Really solid players like Bep Guidolin, Al Arbour, Willie Marshall, and Bill Sweeney also played in the league. And our general manager in Pittsburgh, Baz Bastien, was always in for a practical joke or two.

Once while we were having a bite to eat and a few beers after the game, I looked over at Baz's plate and saw an eye staring up at me, giving me quite a shock. Bastien had a glass eye, which I hadn't known – but of course every player around me was aware of the GM's fake eye. You have to pull one over on the rookie, I guess, and they sure caught me that time!

The time in the AHL made me much more prepared for the NHL than I would have been without it, so I am grateful to all the veteran players and coaches who helped a young kid adjust to the huge jump from junior to professional hockey.

Life was pretty good in Pittsburgh, and I really enjoyed playing there. The city was a nice place, it was clean, and the people were good, hard-working folks. Eleanor and I rented an apartment and met an older couple named the Dabneys, who were really friendly and helped us adjust to life in a new city. The players in the AHL were older and accepting of us, and the league had some great hockey cities, like Hershey and Rochester. The Civic Arena, also known as the Igloo because of its shape, had just been built, so we had a brand-new place to play in. That arena was better than several of the NHL rinks at the time, and we had all the amenities that a big-league team would have.

I would have been happy to stay there all year. I was getting a lot of ice time and it was a positive situation for me. I was called up briefly in November due to some injuries in Detroit, but I really wanted to spend Christmas-time in Pittsburgh, since Eleanor and our first daughter, Heather, were there. I didn't want to be apart from them at that time of year. They agreed, but shortly afterwards I was called up to the NHL for good. After thirty-eight games, ten goals, and twenty-four points, my American Hockey League days were over.

CHAPTER THREE

I WISH I COULD SAY THAT IT WAS A SEAMLESS transition to the NHL for me. But it wasn't. In the American Hockey League, if you asked for help, you'd get it. It was a good place for a young player to ask questions and learn all about the game. In the NHL, there was no one really helping you. For a kid playing in the league at that time, it was a little intimidating. It was very frustrating in a lot of ways, actually.

Being on the buses for week-long road trips in the minors allowed you to bond with your teammates – and the coaching staff, for that matter. In Detroit, both Eleanor and I weren't really treated that well by many of the other players or their wives. I wish I didn't have to say that, but it's true. Sure, it was exciting to be playing in the bigs, but they really made you feel like an outcast until you proved you belonged. It was a real insiders' club, and I wasn't an insider yet. It was not easy to make the NHL in those days, and it was just as tough – if not tougher – to stay there. With only six teams, you were always looking over your shoulder, especially when you first started out. You were always a few bad games away from a demotion to the minors and somebody else taking your job away from you.

NHL general managers would take advantage of that competition too, to keep you on your toes and to keep salaries down. When the league expanded to twelve teams, things started to change big-time on that front, but until then management had players just where they wanted them, and the players knew that.

Bruce MacGregor was a good friend to both of us, though. He and his wife, Audrey, were great to Eleanor and me when we were first coming into the league. We became fast friends and by our second year in Detroit even decided to live across the river in Windsor, where the MacGregors resided.

You had to watch out when you were on the ice too, as nobody on the other teams was going to make it easy for you. I had only been in the National Hockey League for a couple of weeks when we headed to Boston for a game against the Bruins. I had been working on a breakaway play with Doug Barkley in practice, and it had worked pretty well, so I was anxious to try it in a game.

The play was pretty simple and it took advantage of my speed. He'd fire a pass up through centre ice to me and I'd streak off the wing and quickly get behind the defence, then go right in on goal on a breakaway. I hadn't scored a goal up until that point, so Barkley told me he'd look for me when we were on the ice together to try the play.

Well, we were in Boston and I felt the time was right to give the play a try. I noticed that the Bruins had called up some old guy from the minors and teamed him with Leo

Boivin, a solid NHL defenceman who was also getting up there in years by that point.

"Look at those two old farts out there," I said to Barkley. "Have an eye out for me out there coming up the centre. I'm sure it'll work against them."

Nothing special happened in the first period, and in the second period, Barkley saw me on the ice with Boivin and this other guy. He threw a perfect pass right up the centre to me and I took off, head down, to quickly get behind them for the breakaway.

Bang! I had no time to react as Boivin crunched me – and knocked me as cold as a mackerel! I mean, he really clocked me. They brought out the stretcher and wheeled me off, the whole deal.

They used to call Leo Boivin the fire hydrant, as he was just a stocky, hard-hitting defenceman with a solid but short build. But I'd thought he might be too old by now, and maybe too slow, to be able to catch me. I'd thought wrong.

I came to in the dressing room and our trainer, Lefty Wilson, had some ammonia packs under my nose, trying to revive me. He looked at me and asked me if I knew what day it was.

"I could care less what day it is," I replied (or at least that's what I was told I said – I can't really remember). "Just tell me, am I still alive?"

It must have taken me four days to get over that hit. I felt it with every fibre of my body. He just caught me with my head down and hit me the way only Leo Boivin could in his prime.

But you know, I learned a lesson from that hit. I never wound up getting hit that hard again because I learned to

31

keep my head up and be cognizant of who was on the ice at all times. I learned a valuable lesson and applied it – and I also realized that I had better not underestimate an older player ever again, especially a hard hitter like Boivin. Hockey players get hit – it's just a part of the game, and I took a lot of them over the years – but that Boivin hit just about killed me!

It was a good clean hit, though – players back then had respect for each other.

Another thing about Boston: I had the opportunity to play in a lot of great arenas that held a lot of great memories. But some of those great old arenas didn't exactly have the best amenities. The worst place to play for an opposing player? That's an easy question to answer: Boston Garden.

That place was just a joke. You'd walk into the dressing room and there'd be a wooden bench that had to have been an original piece of furniture from when they had opened the place. There was a nail hammered into the wall – that was where you were supposed to hang your clothes.

The floor was solid cement, rock hard. And it wasn't a very clean floor either, for that matter. The conditions really were atrocious. Then you'd get out to the ice and to the players' benches and you'd see more benches that must have been there since the place had opened. There would be jackknife marks in the benches too, with "So and so was here" carved right into them! It was unbelievable.

Chicago wasn't much better, and the old Stadium had those stairs you had to climb up and down, as if you were going into a dungeon. Yes, those old buildings had lots of charm and were great for the fans and atmosphere, but they were hardly great places for visiting teams to play in. When

I see some of the beautiful new arenas in the NHL these days and their luxurious dressing rooms, I wonder what today's players would think about the dressing room the visitors "enjoyed" in the old Boston Garden.

I was used primarily as a penalty killer in that first season, getting the odd shift here and there. I had three goals and three assists in thirty-two games and got to appear in fourteen playoff games, adding another two goals and three assists.

After a fourth-place finish in the regular season, we advanced to the playoffs and stunned Chicago in seven games to go on to the Stanley Cup finals against the Toronto Maple Leafs. It was a great thing to happen to me in my first NHL season. I was excited as I had great bonuses in my contract for making the playoffs and for winning each series, so it was great on a couple of fronts.

We led that final series 3–2, with game six at the Detroit Olympia, with us having a chance to close it out at home. We trailed 1–0 before I scored on a breakaway against Johnny Bower early in the second period to tie it 1–1, by far the biggest goal in my brief NHL career.

Bobby Baun would eventually score the game-winning goal in overtime – one of hockey's great goals since he scored it playing on a broken leg – to tie the series. Toronto then blanked us 4–0 at Maple Leaf Gardens to win the Cup, leaving me in tears. We were just one win away from being able to win a Cup in my rookie year, and we had two chances to get that win!

We had great players on that team, including the great Terry Sawchuk. He was the best goalie of his era, in my mind, and boy was he tough to beat in big games. Bill Gadsby was also terrific, standing up at the blue line and delivering crushing hits to anybody who tried to get in his way. Baun's overtime winner in game six deflected off his stick, however, and it cost him his best chance to win a Stanley Cup. He played for twenty seasons, with Chicago, Detroit, and New York, and he never won a Cup.

Despite the frustrations, it was an exciting period in my life, there is no disputing that. I was playing in the NHL and making some good money. In the playoffs that first year, I drove into the Olympia parking lot in a 1954 Dodge that cost me all of $200! I'll never forget someone yelling at me, "Hey, Henderson! Why don't you just get a horse and buggy?" So of course, I had to get a new car. I bought a 1964 Pontiac Parisienne two-door hardtop, a beautiful car back then, for $3,267. I still have the receipt from that car as a keepsake!

In my second year, 1964–65, I was playing on the fourth line, behind the great Gordie Howe as well as Bruce MacGregor and Floyd Smith. I was still not getting a lot of ice time, but at least I was starting to be accepted as a member of the team because it was clear I was there to stay. I got into all seventy games, picking up eight goals and thirteen assists for twenty-one points and killing penalties, and I'd learned to contribute defensively when called upon.

In addition to the wingers who were ahead of me on the depth chart, we had terrific players and seven future Hall of Famers, like Ted Lindsay, Alex Delvecchio, Norm Ullman, Gordie Howe, Bill Gadsby, Terry Sawchuk, and Marcel Pronovost. There were a lot of great players on that team, but none greater than Howe, of course. There was nobody tougher to play against than Gordie, who could really dish out the punishment, as everybody in hockey knows. I played with him and against him and saw what a fierce competitor he could be.

Lindsay was another all-time great, to be sure. He had been retired for four years after leaving the Chicago Blackhawks when he rejoined us that season. He was forty years old by then and was 170 pounds at the most, but he was still as hard-nosed as ever, picking up 173 minutes in penalties and playing the same rugged style he did in helping Detroit win four Stanley Cups in the 1950s.

Ullman and Delvecchio were top-notch stars, of course, and our acrobatic goalie Roger Crozier was rookie of the year and first-team all-star. Crozier was terrific that first season and became known for his spectacular saves while having some good years in Detroit. We finished first that year with eighty-seven points, but we were upset in the first round of the playoffs by Bobby Hull and Chicago in seven tough games.

The 1965–66 season was a breakthrough year for me, really. After an injury to Ron Murphy, I was moved to left wing for the first time and would wind up playing that position for the next fifteen seasons. Playing on a line with Ullman, I scored twenty-two goals and added twenty-four assists for what was a pretty darn good season in the NHL back then, as there were only nineteen players who scored twenty or more goals in the NHL that season. Ullman, who made it to the Hockey Hall of Fame, was such a pro – what a treat it was to play on a line with him. I started with him that season and stayed with him on a line for basically the rest of my NHL career.

There was no first-place repeat that season, however. We slipped into fourth place with seventy-four points as Montreal claimed first. But we had a great playoff and almost came up with what would have been a huge Stanley Cup upset.

It started in the first round when we knocked out Chicago in six games, the same team that had upset us the year before. Then in the Cup finals against Montreal, we won the first two games at the Montreal Forum and had them on the ropes heading back to Detroit.

We blew that series, however, losing the next four games. Make no mistake about it: Montreal had a great hockey team, but we didn't help our cause by our behaviour in that series. Instead of practising hard and being disciplined, we spent more time in bars and at the racetrack than we should have. The Canadiens were far more focused than we were, and our coach, Sid Abel, couldn't control the team. Abel was a decent guy, but he had a lot on his plate being both GM and coach and he had difficulty relating to a lot of our players.

Henri Richard scored the Cup-winning goal in game six of the series on a controversial goal that looked like it might have gone in off his hand (it sure did to me because I was on the ice at the time!). But the goal stood and we lost the Cup right on Olympia ice, a moment in my career that still bothers me to this day. We were so close, and a little more discipline might have made the difference.

It was a great lifestyle, the life of an NHL player, but it took a bit of getting used to, especially for a kid from Lucknow. I didn't drink until I turned pro, for instance, but, boy, you had to learn to drink if you were going to hang out with NHL players. The biggest surprise of my life was seeing first-hand how much these guys could drink! We'd go out for a team lunch after practice when we were on the road and have a few beers. Then we'd be out for dinner later on and we'd have a few more beers. Some guys knew when to stop, but many didn't and developed problems later on, unfortunately.

NHL salaries back then weren't nearly what they are today – to say the least! – but you could make a very good living playing hockey compared to most other sports, and that certainly made it easy to enjoy life on the road, if that's what you really wanted to do. I was just interested in carving out a good career for myself and my family for as long as I could.

And it was a decent living back then, when you considered the prices of things. There was little negotiating; you just took what they offered you. My first-year contract was for $7,000, which was the NHL minimum, plus a $1,500 signing bonus. When we made the Stanley Cup finals I picked up another $6,500 in bonuses, so that made for a great year financially – $15,000 total. That is a pittance compared to what players are getting today, obviously. But remember what I paid for my car, and I bought my first house for $10,300, so it certainly was a different world economically.

As the years went by, agents became very helpful in contract talks. But when I went back in to negotiate my second deal prior to the 1964–65 season, I really didn't know what to ask for, so I wound up getting what they told me I'd be getting, which was a $1,500 raise. I got the same raise the following season.

By the start of the 1966–67 season, I was looking for more. Sid Abel was the Red Wings' general manager and coach at the time, and he wasn't an easy guy to try to hammer a deal out with. He told me he thought I had done a good job and he was prepared to offer me a $2,500 raise. The thing was, he acted like he was doing me some huge favour by offering me any kind of a raise. I figured I'd played three years in the league and was coming off a twenty-two-goal season – a year when only nineteen guys had scored twenty or more – so I should be up for a lot more than that.

"Well, Sid," I said. "I was thinking of a lot more than that, actually. I was thinking about a $5,000 raise."

I have no idea where I came up with that figure, but I'll never forget his reaction.

"Are you out of your mind, Henderson?!" he bellowed. "You can forget that. You'll take this deal or I'll bury you so far in the minors they won't find you with a shovel!"

So much for stress-free negotiating, I guess! But I figured I had some leverage. The team's owner, Bruce Norris, really wanted to beat Chicago more than any other team, as his brother Jim owned the Hawks. Bruce was an intense competitor, and we were opening up at home against Chicago that season. There was no way he wanted to go into that game without his best lineup, so I thought my best chance to get a better deal was right then and there. I knew our owner would not want to be embarrassed against his brother's team in the home opener. My strategy was simple: Norris's desire to win would take precedence over trying to save more money, and eventually the message would get back to Abel to sign me before the season started. It was all a matter of timing, as far as I was concerned.

The negotiating went on and on, and the raise even got up to $4,000. I have to admit, Eleanor was petrified, telling me to sign the deal. It was a lot of money back then. But I had a feeling that my strategy was sound, and I was playing well in the exhibition games. I truly believed Norris would give in.

Well, our talks went on, right up until the morning of that first game. I had no idea if I'd be playing, as I still hadn't signed, and neither I nor Abel were budging. But finally I was called in by Abel on game day.

He was madder than a you-know-what. But guess what – I got that $5,000! He literally threw a contract at me to sign and said, "Don't tell anybody what you are making!" Well, I didn't, and I also played with gusto to make sure I earned every penny of that contract. Looking back on it, I wished that I had asked Sid if I was right in thinking that Bruce Norris would cave in to my demands in order to win. It would have been interesting to know.

It worked out pretty well for me, and I didn't disappoint. Early that season I scored four goals and made sure they realized they didn't make a mistake in signing me to that kind of a deal.

Hockey sure has changed since then. Players have a lot more say, and with agents and high-priced contracts, well, let's just say that nobody argues over a lousy five grand anymore! You still have holdouts, of course, but the dollar figures are a lot higher. And with all the multi-year contracts in today's game, most players don't have to constantly haggle about their deals like we had to do just about every season.

But that was the way things were done back then. Abel was no different than a lot of other general managers at that time, including the GM I would play for later on, Punch Imlach. Imlach even had a chair in front of his desk with legs he had shortened by several inches. He would ask you to sit in the chair, which was so low to the ground that you'd be looking up at him, a power-play technique he would use during talks. I remember more than once getting up out of that seat, telling him I didn't want to look up at him while we talked. It just felt ridiculous.

I would have a lot of difficult contract talks in future years (like just about every year), so this was a sign of things to come. Players just didn't have the clout back in those days, and you had to look out for yourself because nobody else was going to look after you.

With that negotiation behind me, it was time for the 1966–67 season, which was not a good one for me healthwise, or for the Red Wings, unfortunately. I was hurt for a lot of the season, and it limited me to just forty-six games. I did score twenty-one goals, so I was very productive when I did play, but I had torn chest muscles and groin and knee problems that really held me back, including some breathing problems that required me to go to Arizona for a few weeks.

We missed the playoffs that year, and we had one issue after another, it seemed. Doug Barkley's career came to an end when he took a stick to the eye, and that was devastating to him and the team, as he had a chance to be one of the best defencemen in hockey. Marcel Pronovost was dealt to Toronto and Bill Gadsby retired, so that really hurt our defence. We seemed to be on the downside in a hurry, after making it to the finals just the year prior.

I was healthier at the start of the 1967–68 season, but our defence was in shambles in the first year of the expanded, twelve-team NHL. We allowed a league-high 257 goals, more even than the six expansion teams.

So I guess that something had to give. And something did, and it was big – and it involved me.

CHAPTER FOUR

I LOVED PLAYING IN DETROIT. I WAS PLAYING WELL, I felt we had a pretty good hockey team, and all in all, life was going fine for me. My career was really just starting, and I was able to produce.

How could I not love playing in Detroit? I was only a kid – I was more awestruck than anything else. The city itself really didn't do anything special for me, and we spent most of our time in Windsor after we moved there anyway. But the atmosphere in the arena was tremendous, and the rink was filled every night.

They had great hockey fans in Detroit, with a real passion for the game. It was the six-team era of the National Hockey League (up until expansion in 1967, of course), and tickets were a scarce commodity. It was very lucrative for me too; the Red Wings had a tremendous bonus structure, and in my first few years there, we went to the finals and semifinals, so the extra money certainly helped. But even though the money was good – and I needed it with a young family to look after – primarily I was just so thrilled at being able to play in the National Hockey League. Every day, I had to pinch myself because I had made it to the best league in the world. "Holy moly!" I would say to myself, looking around that dressing room. "There's Gordie Howe. There's Bill Gadsby. I'm actually playing with these guys." I thought I was in heaven.

We really had nothing in Lucknow, and now I had everything in Detroit. I'd be sitting in the dressing room and we'd be talking back and forth during intermissions, and Gordie Howe might say to me, "Nice play there, Henny. Way to go!" Just imagine how good that would make a kid like me feel. Whenever somebody said that to me, I'd always think, "Where's my dad? He should be hearing this," and wished I had a tape recorder so I could have him listen to it! It was such a fantastic time for me.

Detroit was a great sports town, and a winning sports town. Since the 1930s, it has been known as the City of Champions. The baseball Tigers were doing well, and would win the World Series in 1968. The Lions had won three National Football League championships in the 1950s and had a fiercely loyal following. The University of Michigan, in nearby Ann Arbor, won the Rose Bowl one year. It could also be a tough city, and it was going through a difficult time with all the violence and the riots in the summer of 1967, but inside the Olympia the fans were great. It really was a great environment.

Outside the arena was something else, though! After practice, we would always stop by a convenience store on the corner where the Olympia was. We'd get a pop or whatever, and one day, Gary Bergman left his brand-new

Chevy running while he went inside. Sure enough, while he was in the store, some kid just came along and drove off with that new car!

But for a kid coming into the NHL from a place like Lucknow, stuff like that didn't matter. I was just happy to be in the NHL, and I was very happy being a Detroit Red Wing.

Then, on March 3, 1968, the unthinkable happened. The Red Wings dealt me to the Toronto Maple Leafs, along with centre Norm Ullman and right-winger Floyd Smith. In exchange, the Wings got left-winger Frank Mahovlich, centre Peter Stemkowski, rookie Garry Unger, and the NHL rights to former Leafs defenceman Carl Brewer, who had joined the Canadian National Team and by now was playing in the International Hockey League with Muskegon. It was, at the time – and probably still is when you think about it – one of the biggest trades in hockey history.

That deal is still talked about to this day, as it involved a lot of prime-time players. Imlach was always fond of veteran players, but when you fell out of favour with him, you were quite often on the way out of town. Mahovlich clearly needed a change of scenery, and the Wings wanted to shake things up as well, so both teams were willing to make a blockbuster deal.

I found out when Audrey MacGregor, Bruce's wife, heard it on the radio and then told all of us! What a way to find out that you've been uprooted and you are on your way to play in another city. Sid Abel contacted me eventually and apologized, saying they meant to tell us directly, but I was hurt so bad I don't think I even heard a word he said.

I was so let down. I had never felt rejection before, and I hated the feeling I had in my gut. I was disappointed and angry; I couldn't believe that this had happened. I'll never forget playing Detroit for the first time after the deal, at Maple Leaf Gardens, and winning 5–3. I had a goal and an assist and was the second star of the game that night. That certainly made me feel a lot better about the trade, especially after the way I felt at first.

But as is often the case in life, things that happen to you that you think are not good for you turn out to be very beneficial for you in the long run. I went on to have some good years in Toronto – good enough, of course, to earn me a spot on what turned out to be the Team of the Century just a few years after that.

The trade hurt me deeply, as I said, and I wasn't the least bit happy about going to the Maple Leafs at first. I had nothing against them, I just didn't want to be traded anywhere; I was naive enough to think that I'd be playing in Detroit my entire playing career.

But after the shock wore off, I came to enjoy playing at Maple Leaf Gardens. There was something really special about playing in that building, and maybe it had to do with the crowd. Back in the 1960s and 1970s when I was playing, people came to the games in a shirt and tie. And I mean most everybody dressed up. There was a real sense of class about the place on a game night. I guess the fans dressing up like that showed a respect for the game, gave it a certain dignity. It made it feel like something important was going on inside that arena on game night.

It's funny, though. I'd never thought too much about playing in Maple Leaf Gardens until I got there. I'd grown up in southern Ontario, and just like everybody else, I always knew what Maple Leaf Gardens represented, but the full impact of playing there on a regular basis didn't hit me until I became a Toronto Maple Leaf.

On top of everything else, you knew that half of Canada would be watching you on a Saturday night on *Hockey Night in Canada*. Now *that* was pressure, but it was also the brightest spotlight you could play under. It's one of the reasons I think that so many players on the visiting teams had their best games in the Gardens: because they knew everybody would be watching, including all their family and friends. And when you combine that with the crowd dressed to the nines, the bright lights – well, how could you not love playing in that building?

The place suited my personality too. I liked the spotlight, and the pressure, of playing in that place. Maybe when I got older and had lost a step, it was good to be away from such scrutiny, but nothing beat playing in Maple Leaf Gardens, one of the great arenas of all time.

The Leafs had won the Stanley Cup the year before my arrival, but now the team was going through a remake, as they were an older group. Montreal and Chicago were as strong as ever, while Boston and New York, who had fought over last place for most of the 1960s, were evolving into powerful teams. Meanwhile, we had a strong nucleus in players like Dave Keon, Ron Ellis, Norm Ullman, and Mike Walton, and a group of rising young defenceman like Jim Dorey, Pat Quinn, and Mike Pelyk. Later on, the team added Rick Ley, Brad Selwood, Jim McKenny, and Brian Glennie, so if management did its job, this was a team with a lot of promise for the future.

I played on a line with Ullman and Smith, two of my former teammates in Detroit, and had eleven points in the thirteen games left in the regular season schedule, but we still missed the playoffs.

In 1968–69, we bounced back to grab a playoff spot with eighty-five points, ending up fourth in the East Division. But the playoffs were a disaster, as we were swept by the Bruins with Bobby Orr and Phil Esposito in four straight games, losing the first two games in Boston 10–0 and 7–0. We were no match for the Bruins in that series, which featured the monstrous hit on Orr by Pat Quinn in Boston Garden. Right after the final game, Punch Imlach, who had been with the team since 1958, was fired as general manager and coach.

Imlach's firing was so sudden. It was a bit of a shock the way they did it. However, I have to say we weren't terribly surprised that Punch lost his job. He had a tough situation going on with the Leafs at that time. The team was rebuilding, and the roster was in transition, so it wasn't the best place to be for any general manager and coach right about then. In the dressing room, we all knew there was no way we could compete against the better teams in the league, as we had shown in that series against Boston.

I didn't wind up playing very long for Imlach, but he was certainly a very different coach than Abel was in Detroit. You just couldn't challenge Imlach; he couldn't stand anyone challenging him at any time. He was in total control of his teams, and you had better listen to him – or else. Abel was the opposite in that respect; he didn't have an ego problem and was easier to talk to.

However, there was no doubt that Imlach had his strengths. He understood hockey, and he was a very good strategist. He was sharp at matching lines during a game, and was a very good tactician. He got more out of that 1967 Stanley

Cup Leafs team than anyone else could have, as that team probably shouldn't have won a Stanley Cup. The Leafs really shouldn't have beaten us (the Red Wings) back in 1963 either, but he did another good job with that team. But he got the most out of many of his players.

I remember that when I came to the team, he gave me Norman Vincent Peale's famous book *The Power of Positive Thinking* – he really believed in it. I did too – some people kidded me that I could have written that book. That was Imlach's upside: the positive thinking really came through when some of his teams won despite not being as talented as the opponents they beat.

His downside was his arrogance and his superstition. He had one flavour for everybody – he just couldn't deal with players who were more idiosyncratic. He couldn't understand them. Players like Frank Mahovlich, Carl Brewer, and Mike "Shaky" Walton, for instance – they just weren't Imlach's kind of players. If he had been a little wiser and a little more of a communicator, he would have been an even better coach.

And he was superstitious – very superstitious. That really drove me crazy, and a lot of other players wondered what he was up to as well. He'd wear the same hat because it was lucky, send players down to Rochester on a gut feeling, and make some hockey decisions based on superstition. When you operate like that, you lose a lot of respect in some quarters, and I think that really hurt Punch.

By the end of that 1969 playoff series, the writing was on the wall, and most of us knew it. He didn't deserve to be fired in such a quick and heartless way, but as I said, he was in a very tough spot and we really weren't shocked that they made a coaching change.

The 1969–70 season was very disappointing for us. Johnny McLellan took over as coach of the Leafs, and was as nice a man as you'd ever meet, but was probably too nice to be a coach in the NHL. People often took advantage of his kind nature, and that made a tough job even tougher. He was in a difficult spot, as he didn't inherit a very good team, especially after we dealt Tim Horton – who had turned forty, but had been a first-team all-star in 1968–69 – to the New York Rangers. New general manager Jim Gregory put his mark on the team right away, but it wasn't enough to salvage the season. We finished last in the East Division with seventy-one points, and I managed twenty goals and twenty-two assists for forty-two points. I was severely hampered by a groin problem that season. It was so bad that by the end of the year my right thigh was an inch and a half bigger than my left because I was essentially skating on one leg all year. I shouldn't have been in the lineup, but I wanted to play so badly that I didn't take the time off to heal properly, and the Leafs really wanted me to stay in the lineup. That would never happen today – NHL trainers and players now realize how damaging it can be to any player to play through an injury that needs time to heal, but at that time there was a lot of pressure to keep on playing.

That off-season meant time for a new contract, which certainly wasn't the best timing for me, and the Leafs management knew it. They sent me a contract offer in the mail that had a raise of just $1,500.

Jim Gregory and King Clancy called me after they sent it and basically said they didn't think I should get much of a raise since my offensive numbers were down. That got me steaming! I reminded them that I had played hurt all year with the groin injury and shouldn't even have been playing. I really couldn't believe that they would overlook such an obvious reason for my decline in production and offer me such a small raise.

They apologized and came back with a better offer, but I never forgot the slight. It convinced me beyond a doubt that hockey was just a business and management would only look after me if it was in their best interests. From then on, I realized that only Paul Henderson would look after Paul Henderson.

The Leafs were basically turning over completely from the team that had won four Stanley Cups in six years. George Armstrong, "The Chief," was the captain of those great teams, Dave Keon was a huge star, and the incomparable Johnny Bower was in goal. We still had Armstrong and Keon, but they were all that remained from the dynasty days.

There have been a lot of great captains and leaders in the history of the Toronto Maple Leafs over the years, and George Armstrong was our very capable captain during this time. His "Chief" nickname came from his native roots, but it also described what a presence he was in the locker room and on the ice for more than two decades in the NHL, a good portion of that as Leafs captain.

I always respected George on the ice when I played against him. He was a battler who played the game hard but fairly. When I got to Toronto, though, I was impressed to discover just how competitive he was. He sure came to play every night and had no patience for those players who didn't.

But George was certainly a different cat. I saw him not that long ago at a Toronto Maple Leafs game, and he was as colourful as always. I asked him, "George, how is Betty [his wife] doing?" And he said, "I can't get her to die! I keep saying to her, 'When are you going to die?'" I know how much George loves his wife, so I just laugh at comments like that, but that's George. I mean, who says that about his wife?! He's a very different character, that's for sure.

And oddly enough, even though he's so outgoing and friendly when you see him in a press box, scouting, or wherever, he never gives interviews and has never even been to the Hall of Fame – and he's a member! He just doesn't think he truly belongs there and he stays away. Like I said, he's different in a lot of ways, but a good man and a capable captain.

Dave Keon was one of the most finicky people I've ever seen, especially when it came to his equipment. He couldn't stand anything not being exactly as he wanted it to be, and he wouldn't play until everything was just right for him. But he was a leader by example, with an impeccable work ethic, and maybe one of the best forecheckers of his era. He literally danced on his skates with what appeared to be complete ease and effortlessness, and that drove us crazy, wondering how he could be so light on his skates.

Johnny Bower was both a great player and a great guy. There was nobody else like him. Johnny didn't even make the NHL to stay until he was thirty-four – at least as far as we know, because he lied about his age so often nobody was certain just how old he was! – but, boy, did he ever make up for lost time. He was a tremendous goalie in big games and was an integral part of several Toronto Stanley Cup winners.

Johnny is the kind of guy who is always there to help other people, and he is dearly loved by everyone who knows him. He's helped so many charitable causes over the years, and he seldom says no to anybody. Only recently has he slowed down even just a little, and he is always the consummate humble gentleman. But when he was playing goal – man, he couldn't stand anybody getting the puck past him, even in practices!

The remarkable thing is that Johnny doesn't have a clue just how great a goalie he was. He was and still is today so humble. You seldom meet a man who is more down to earth than Johnny Bower. Everybody loves Johnny, and with good reason. He is certainly finishing well, as I like to say.

We rebounded to finish fourth in the East Division in 1970–71, with eighty-two points. I played on a line with Norm Ullman and Ron Ellis and enjoyed my best season to date in the NHL, with thirty goals and thirty assists. Over the next two seasons, we comprised a solid line that could compete with any in the NHL. We were also very good defensively; our two-way game made us that much more effective.

That season also saw Darryl Sittler join our team after being drafted eighth overall in the 1970 draft, and it was easy to see how determined he was to become an NHL star – few players worked harder than he did. He developed into an incredible team leader during his career. We were both small-town boys and had a lot in common, and we enjoyed each other's company, especially when we both bought homes in Mississauga. During the 1972 series against the Soviet Union, Darryl and his wife, Wendy, looked after our three daughters while Eleanor and I were in Moscow. Darryl, of course, went on to become one of the best players in NHL history and, in 1989, was inducted into the Hockey Hall of Fame.

RON ELLIS ON PLAYING WITH HENDERSON AND ULLMAN

Those years with the Toronto Maple Leafs were tough in a lot of ways. We didn't win a lot of games, and we missed the playoffs a lot. We didn't have nearly as much success as we would have hoped. But they were still good years in a lot of ways too because I got to play with two great players, Paul Henderson and Normie Ullman. It was remarkable, really, when you think about it, because we played together for six years, I guess, and we all produced equally. Usually, there's one guy on a line who is the big scorer, but we all had such similar totals. I think that's because we complemented each other so well. Paul was the kind of player who took chances – he liked to stay deep and look for that turnover or scoring chance – while Norm Ullman was such a good forechecker, so tenacious, always forcing the play. As for me, well, my role was that those guys knew I always had their backs. I would look after the defensive side and do my part when needed. We were a real line and we worked well together. I think that's why we enjoyed playing with each other and had so much success as a unit over the years. It really was a pleasure playing with them. Those years with Paul and Norm in Toronto were the most enjoyable years of my life.

We were solid in goal as well. We picked up one of the all-time greats, Jacques Plante, in a trade with St. Louis, and later in 1970–71 we got Bernie Parent, as good a young goalie as there was in the league at that time, in a deal with Philadelphia. Bobby Baun, who had been claimed by California in the 1967 expansion draft, came back to Toronto early in the season. Although he was older, at thirty-four, he was just as tough as ever and really contributed with his crushing bodychecks. Baun could block shots with the best of them and was a warrior who never backed off when he was on the ice. He was a real help to our younger defencemen on the team too, a real role model for them by the way he played.

Despite those additions, we lost out in the playoffs again, dropping a six-game series to the Rangers. That was a hard-fought series and we competed, but we just didn't have the depth to beat the better teams in the league. Harold Ballard hated spending money, and if he had, we might have been a much better team. But he didn't have to spend an extra dime, since the Gardens was filled every night.

I hit another personal best in 1971–72 by scoring thirty-eight goals in seventy-three games. With Boston, New York, and Montreal all cracking the 100-point barrier, the best we could hope for, though, was another fourth-place finish, with eighty points.

McLellan got sick that year and was replaced by King Clancy for a stretch. It was a great run for King, as we went 9–3–3 while under his reign, and even though his time as a top-flight hockey strategist had passed, he was a funny and charming man and kept us loose and winning.

It was another early playoff exit, as the powerful Boston Bruins, led by Bobby Orr and Phil Esposito, took us out in five games. We still didn't have the depth we needed. But we had a solid core, I was playing some of the best hockey of my career, and there seemed to be a lot to look forward to once the 1972–73 season came around – if Ballard didn't screw it all up, and believe me, that was always a possibility!

But first, there would be the little matter of taking care of some business with the Soviet Union.

CHAPTER FIVE

THE SUMMER OF 1972 WAS A GOOD TIME IN MY LIFE. I was coming off a very solid season with the Maple Leafs, and Eleanor and I were looking forward to a trip overseas. An auto parts company, AP Parts, that I was doing some work for in the off-season was taking us and twenty-five other couples on a European river cruise down the Rhine River. It sounded like a fun trip, and Eleanor and I were looking forward to it.

Well, we wound up travelling overseas, of course, but to the Soviet Union – and it certainly was no vacation.

I guess I should first provide a little background on how much the Russians were dominating in world hockey at that point.

Canada had always been the power in international hockey, of course, as it was our country's national game. As the years went on, a few things happened. First, European nations started playing the game a lot more and a lot better. Their game emphasized speed and skill with less focus on physicality, and playing on the bigger ice surfaces over there certainly helped.

The second thing that happened was that in both the world championships and the Olympics, Canada sent only amateur players, not professionals. The Soviet Union was producing great players, many of whom could – and should – have played in the NHL. In the days of the Iron Curtain, however, that wasn't possible.

So the Russians took over on the international scene, as their top players wound up playing against our amateurs in all the major events, which was hardly fair to Canadian hockey.

The Russians were great players, make no mistake about that, and they were really improving as a hockey nation. That, combined with the fact that Canada didn't send its best players to international competition, led to the Soviet Union dominating world and Olympic competition from 1956 until 1972.

From 1920 until 1963, Canada usually sent the most recent Allan Cup championship teams. Following the 1963 world championships, Father David Bauer founded the Canadian National Team to take over that role. Canada withdrew from official International Ice Hockey Federation (IIHF) events in 1970, and the national team program was suspended after we were refused permission to use even semi-professional players at the world championship.

It was against this backdrop that hockey officials in Canada and the Soviet Union decided to play a "super series" that would pit the best players Canada had to offer against the best players from Russia in an eight-game series that would take place in September 1972.

So much has been written and said about that series over the years, and justifiably so. It was a huge deal back then, all across the country. As players in the National Hockey League, we knew what was at stake and we knew what an honour it would be to play in that series. It was the first time that the best players in the Soviet Union would play the best players from Canada in an international series, so we were all pretty pumped about it. We really wanted to finally put those Ruskies in their place!

But honestly, I didn't think it would be much of a series. The best players in the world were from Canada, we all believed that. I certainly did. And it's not that I thought the Russians weren't any good. We knew they were good. But I thought we'd win just because of all the firepower we had. I thought we would overwhelm them. There was no way any team was going to beat us. We were all pretty confident of that.

I thought they might tie one game, or maybe win once, but I felt that if we didn't win at least seven games it would be a travesty. And I wasn't the only person in the country who was thinking that either.

It was the job of head coach Harry Sinden and his assistant, John Ferguson, to pick the team, and they had a lot of options to choose from. I felt I'd at least get invited to the camp, after scoring thirty-eight goals the year before. I always took care of myself in the summer, was always in shape, and after some initial reservations cancelled our holiday cruise so I could attend Team Canada's training camp.

Early that summer I got a letter officially inviting me to camp, so I was ready to go. I knew it would be tough to make that team, as almost everybody who was invited was an all-star. We had incredible firepower up front. Phil Esposito, Jean Ratelle, Stan Mikita, Red Berenson, Gilbert Perreault, Marcel Dionne, and Bobby Clarke were the centres – how is that for depth! Frank Mahovlich, Pete Mahovlich, Rod Gilbert, Yvan Cournoyer, Mickey Redmond, Vic Hadfield, and Rick Martin were all high-scoring wingers, and our defence corps included names like Brad Park, Bill White, Pat Stapleton, Guy Lapointe, Don Awrey, Rod Seiling, Gary Bergman, and Serge Savard. We also had plenty of other solid players on defence and up front who could fill a variety of roles, and Ken Dryden, Tony Esposito, and Eddie Johnston gave us very solid goaltending.

We wouldn't have such stars as Bobby Hull, J.C. Tremblay, Gerry Cheevers, or Derek Sanderson because they had all jumped to the World Hockey Association, and we were missing the legendary Bobby Orr, who tried to play but couldn't due to a knee injury. But when players like Johnny Bucyk and Dave Keon couldn't even merit an invitation to training camp, there was no reason not to think we would have a tremendous team that could beat anybody in the world.

One of the toughest things we had to watch at the Summit Series was Bobby Orr's attempt to play for Canada. Orr was the greatest defenceman of his era by far, a game-changer. He controlled the pace of hockey games, he could do everything, and we were all hoping against hope that he'd be able to play for us.

He came to training camp, but it became evident pretty quickly that he was in too much pain and couldn't function after all the crippling knee injuries and surgeries he'd had.

There's no doubt that Bobby was devastated. And it was tough to see him sitting in the stands, watching us, knowing that he couldn't get out there. And after our loss in game one, let me tell you, we were all saying, "Where's Bobby Orr? We could really use him now!"

It might have been a very different series with him in the lineup – we'll never know. But we do know what a shame it was that Orr couldn't have taken part in such a historic event. You had to feel for him – and feel for us for not being able to use him against the Russians.

I was pleased that my teammate and linemate with the Maple Leafs Ron Ellis was also there. We knew how to play together, and when they put us on a line with Bobby Clarke, we seemed to hit it off together as a unit. We were kept as a line right from the very start.

We came to training camp dead serious, and the three of us were ready to play. We worked our tails off and realized very early in the camp that, while we were long shots to form one of the top lines, we were going to make the team and contribute. We felt we were the best line at camp in the early going. We were fast, we could all hurt you offensively, and were responsible defensively as well. We might have started as the fifth, sixth, or even seventh line, but we came there with a purpose and we wanted to prove we could play with the best players in the world.

It was obvious at camp that some of the other guys weren't as prepared and didn't take it as seriously as we did. Everybody on Team Canada was a star on his own team, and some of them were being asked to fill roles and do things they weren't used to doing. And some would be asked to play only sparingly and sit out some games because we had such a large roster. It was management's feeling that we needed a lot of players because we were playing in the off-season and some guys wouldn't be in the greatest shape, so everyone would end up getting a chance to play.

It didn't work out that way, as some guys didn't get to play at all. We all had to adapt and learn to play together in a hurry. The only line that played together on a regular basis in the NHL was the Rod Gilbert–Vic Hadfield–Jean Ratelle unit, so the rest of us had to find at least one new linemate and try to make it work quickly. Ron and I were really lucky – our line clicked early in the camp, while other combinations struggled.

RON ELLIS ON PLAYING WITH HENDERSON AND CLARKE

We were the only line that stayed together for all eight games in the series. We had such great players at that training camp and on our roster, so for us to have stayed together for the entire series was an amazing thing. But really, looking back on it now, I can see how we were able to do it. First of all, Paul and I were friends and we'd played together for several years by then and were comfortable together. With Team Canada, they picked Bobby Clarke to play on the line with us and he was the kind of player that fit with Paul and me perfectly. In a lot of ways he was just a younger version of Norm Ullman, a great playmaker and tenacious forechecker who would do anything to win. Paul and I didn't have to change our game one bit against the Russians thanks to pairing us with Bobby Clarke, so it really did work out for the best for us. We were a real line right from the get-go.

Despite the problems in managing such a large roster, I think if we had to do it all over again we'd have picked the same guys. Maybe some guys didn't work quite hard enough to merit playing time, or maybe some guys just couldn't find the right linemates. Whatever the case, you are always going to have some issues when you have that many stars all together. They picked the right players for this huge assignment, no doubt in my mind.

In the Red–White game, I scored twice and Clarke scored once in a 5–3 win for our team that really cemented us as one of the top lines as the series drew near. The series would open at the Montreal Forum, and we felt as ready as we could be.

How wrong we were about that.

In the dressing room at the Forum before game one, we were like caged animals. We were so pumped up it was crazy. Everyone in the country had been talking about this series for so long that we were at a fever pitch, eager to finally get at it.

We charged out onto the ice and the place was electric. We couldn't wait to get going and run all over the Russians and prove Canadian hockey superiority once and for all. We were all tired of the Russians claiming to be better and beating Canadians at other international events because we didn't send our best players.

Prime Minister Pierre Trudeau dropped the puck for the ceremonial faceoff and the first game was finally underway. Phil Esposito was so charged up that he won that ceremonial faceoff and almost fired the puck all the way back into our own end, that's how much the juices were flowing!

And the start of the game went according to the script we had planned. Esposito scored just thirty seconds into the game, swatting a shot past Vladislav Tretiak, and at 6:32, Clarke got the puck to Ellis off the draw and he dropped it to me. I slapped a quick shot low just inside the post and beat him again, and we were up 2–0.

I'm sure the entire country was going nuts. The Forum sure was! And I'm positive that most fans and media thought this series was going to be a joke, that the Canadians were going to run all over the Russians in a rout. But those of us on the ice with that 2–0 lead knew even then that this was going to be a long series – we saw a tsunami in the background and it was coming right at us.

These Russians were good! They were so composed. We thought they'd just be awestruck by us and collapse, but they weren't the least bit fazed even being down by two goals so quickly. They just kept coming – their physical conditioning was unnerving.

And they scored soon after to get right back into the game. They just kept coming in droves, and looking back on it now, we had expended too much energy in the dressing room before the game. Also, we were nowhere near the physical shape needed to play against this well-oiled machine. Right from the start, we realized their physical conditioning was vastly superior to ours.

How bad was it? It was like getting into a fight and becoming so tired that you couldn't throw another punch if you're life depended on it. We would come back to the bench and be so out of breath it was hard to have a conversation. We knew the game was slipping away from us and it was – and it did. We wound up losing the opener by a 7–3 score.

The gory details are well known: we got hammered. And in stunned silence in the Forum the game ended, and we knew now that this series was going to be anything but a cakewalk. What a terrible feeling that was.

The country was stunned – absolutely stunned – after that opening-game loss, but there was little time to stew over it. Two nights after that debacle, we were back at it with a chance to even up the series and make amends. Game two in the series was played at Maple Leaf Gardens, and for obvious reasons I was really looking forward to it. I would be playing in front of my mother and other family and friends in the Leafs' home arena, and we were all looking forward to this game to right the ship in this series.

There was a lot of nervousness, too, because we knew there were going to be changes to the lineup; there had to be. We needed to be a lot more defensive than we were in game one, and we needed to be grittier.

And frankly, some of the guys we had out there just couldn't keep up. Out went Jean Ratelle, Rod Gilbert, Vic Hadfield, Rod Seiling, and Don Awrey; in went Wayne Cashman, J.P. Parise, Stan Mikita, Bill Goldsworthy, and Serge Savard. Tony Esposito replaced Ken Dryden in goal.

The pressure was really on, of course, but we were a lot more composed for that game. There was more of a sense of professionalism in the room before the game, that we had a job to do, and come hell or high water, we were going to do it.

It was another tough game, going back and forth, but it was a much more solid one from our standpoint. We started well and outplayed the Russians in the opening period, but the game was still scoreless after the first twenty minutes.

We didn't get discouraged by that and stayed patient. Phil Esposito finally scored a goal from the slot on a delayed penalty at 7:14 of the second period to open the scoring, setting off a great celebration on the ice and in the stands.

Getting the first goal in that game was crucial for us; it really lifted our spirits.

Yvan Cournoyer then used his blinding speed at 1:19 of the third period to breeze past the Russian defence and snap a shot past Tretiak to give us a 2–0 lead, and we were all feeling much better. But when Alexander Yakushev slipped a rebound past Tony Esposito four minutes later, the heat was on again – especially after Pat Stapleton took a penalty right after that.

It was then that Peter Mahovlich scored one of the most beautiful and important short-handed goals in hockey history. He took a pass from Espo and made a great move on a Russian defenceman before deking Tretiak to complete a remarkable individual effort and make it a 3–1 game. It was such a terrific play that we all leapt off the bench to congratulate him as the Gardens crowd went crazy.

Frank Mahovlich later scored to make it 4–1, and we had the win we so desperately needed. We knew by now that the series was going to be a real dogfight, but at least we were back to square one and we had a real sense of relief in the dressing room.

It was a very satisfying win for me personally, especially in front of the home crowd. And it was really important for our team's state of mind to be headed to Winnipeg for game three with the series tied.

That was a game we led by two goals in – twice – but couldn't close out. It was one of those games where we were just a little too lackadaisical at the wrong times and it cost us dearly. We committed several turnovers and the Soviets pounced on them, but I really felt we should have won that game.

J.P. Parise opened the scoring for us, and after the Russians tied it, Ratelle put us ahead once again before the period ended. Phil Esposito with yet another goal made it 3–1 for Canada at 4:19 of the second period, but Valeri Kharlamov again brought the Russians back to within one. I then fired a slap shot from the top of the right faceoff circle just inside the left goal post to beat Tretiak to again give us a two-goal lead at 4–2, but unfortunately we allowed the Russians to creep back with two more goals before the second period ended.

The third period was scoreless, so the Russians had another point and the series was again tied. Boy, that was a frustrating night in a lot of ways. We felt we let that game get away.

The Russians were tougher than we had expected, especially Tretiak. He was playing a lot better than we'd thought he was capable of before the series, and to this point was probably as good as either of our two goalies had been. We had a lot of great goal scorers, but they were having a lot of trouble beating Tretiak.

We had one more game to play in Canada – two nights later in Vancouver – and despite the bitter disappointment of blowing the leads in game three, we felt to a man that if we could win this game we'd be in pretty good shape.

The coaching staff thought it was a pivotal game as well, making more changes to try to avert another collapse. Dryden was brought back in to replace Tony Esposito, who had been playing very well, and Gilbert, Goldsworthy, Dennis Hull, Vic Hadfield, Rod Seiling, Awrey, and Gilbert Perreault were added at the expense of Ratelle, Mikita, Parise, Cashman, Peter Mahovlich, Lapointe, and Savard. Those changes raised a few eyebrows, but there was pressure on the coaches to get everybody into the lineup at least once. And we had played so poorly in blowing the leads in Winnipeg, so maybe they were warranted.

That fourth game was a bad one for us. We just couldn't seem to get anything going, and I had a really bad feeling as it went on. We were never in this one, and I felt we didn't have any jump at all.

Goldsworthy wound up taking two minor penalties early and the Russians took advantage on the power play to lead 2–0. Perreault scored a nice goal to get us back to within one in the second period, but two more goals by the Russians restored their two-goal lead. Goldsworthy redeemed himself a little by scoring after that, but another Russian goal followed by a marker by Dennis Hull made the final 5–3 Russia, which was a flattering score for us.

It was not a good performance. We had been soundly outplayed, and worst of all, we were booed by the fans in Vancouver throughout the game – basically booed off the ice. It was a horrible ending to the game.

It was then that Phil Esposito made his famous speech to the country when interviewed on CTV after the game. Esposito was such a leader, and his leadership was never more on display than it was after that game.

"To the people of Canada, I say we tried," Esposito said. "We did our best. We're really disheartened, disappointed, and disillusioned. We can't believe we're getting booed in our own building. I'm really, really disappointed. I can't believe it. Some of our guys are really down in the dumps. They have a good team. Let's face facts. We came because we love Canada. I don't think it's fair that we should be booed."

We of course didn't hear Phil's speech since we were in the

dressing room. We sure heard about it later, however, and it became a rallying point for us and all Canadians, but right after that game the mood in our dressing room was pretty grim. We were embarrassed, and frankly, there was a real pity party going on. A lot of guys were moaning about the fact that they had given up their summer only to be booed off the ice. Didn't these fans know we were trying?!

The situation was critical at that point. We were now headed to Sweden to play two exhibition games before the series would resume with four more games in Russia and we were in real trouble. We had been so engrossed in the series that I had really never even thought about the fact that in order to win the series now, we'd have to go to Russia and find a way to get this thing turned around – and we now trailed 2–1–1.

There was a lot of dissension, a lot of infighting among the guys. We were carrying a lot of players – we had to because they had all come to training camp and made themselves available – and everybody was really feeling the heat at this point.

As we went overseas, it was clear we would have to find some solutions in a hurry.

CHAPTER SIX

BEFORE THE GAMES IN MOSCOW, WE STOPPED IN Stockholm, Sweden, for a pair of exhibition games against the Swedish national team. Those games gave us a chance to work on our conditioning, which was very important, and to get used to the bigger ice surface that we'd be playing on over there. We defeated Sweden 4–1 in the first game – I had a goal and an assist in that one – and we played to an ugly 4–4 tie in the second, a tilt that was full of dirty shots and some really rough play. I sat that one out because I was still nursing a sore groin from earlier in the series. For whatever reason, that second game brought out the ugly side of both teams, as we hammered the Swedes physically and they responded with their sticks. It was a clash of styles; in the NHL, we played a hard-hitting style, while European hockey wasn't nearly as physical but was still dirty. But those games helped us get our act together before we got to Moscow, giving us some more conditioning that we needed before the series resumed.

Another reason the games in Sweden were good for us is that we saw first-hand how international refereeing was very different from the kind of officiating we were used to in the National Hockey League. There was no consistency to the calls, and we realized pretty quickly that if we continued to play the hard-hitting NHL style over there, we were going to spend a lot of time killing penalties.

Tempers frayed quickly in those games, but as far as Ronnie Ellis, Bobby Clarke, and I were concerned, we just wanted to keep our noses clean and not upset the apple cart. We were playing well and we knew we'd be playing in Moscow; there were still some other decisions to be made about some of the other guys' ice time, so for them it was different. We were happy with the way we were playing and expected to have a prominent role once the series resumed.

We did come closer together as a unit during those games, and we needed to. Some players had been in open rebellion against Harry Sinden for a while, and they were trying to get him fired right in the middle of the series. They weren't even dealing with Harry by then; they were going straight to Alan Eagleson, so it wasn't a very peaceful time in the dressing room, to be sure.

We did lose four players in Moscow, however. Vic Hadfield, Rick Martin, Gilbert Perreault, and Jocelyn Guevremont all decided to return home. Martin and Guevremont hadn't played a game to that point, and Hadfield had only been used sparingly in a pair of games. Perreault was very unhappy with the limited amount of ice time that he was getting. They likely realized they wouldn't be playing much, if at all, in Russia since our lineup now had pretty much been determined, so they made the decision to leave the team.

It was hard to criticize them, as I know that if I hadn't been playing I would have been going crazy with frustration. Great players like Marcel Dionne, Dale Tallon, Mickey Redmond, Eddie Johnston, and Brian Glennie weren't playing much or at all either, but they stayed and contributed as much as they could, even if it was only as cheerleaders. Other players just couldn't take being in that role.

Still, we were becoming a team by that point, we could all feel it. Sinden was great at keeping us focused on each individual game.

"Just worry about winning game five, and the rest of the series will take care of itself," Sinden told us. He was cool and professional and offset his assistant coach John Ferguson well, as Fergie was far more emotional. But they made a great pair and kept us on track despite the enormous pressure and challenge we were facing.

The Russians were certainly going to make it as difficult as possible for us. We were absolutely surprised at how spartan our accommodations were and how they treated us when we arrived.

It was sort of hilarious, actually. Our wives had come over ahead of us and discovered that all the rooms, for instance, had two single beds . . . and they were positioned head to head in the rooms! Eleanor told them, "This is not going to work with my husband," and she had the beds moved together, side by side. Talk about mind games.

There was what amounted to a warden stationed on every floor of the hotel, and we had to leave our key with them whenever we left. They were all about control, and they were in control in that hotel. The food was . . . well, let's just say it was pretty mediocre at best and the rest of the time downright awful! Eleanor grew up on a farm and knew a rotten egg when she saw one – and one morning at breakfast we were served an egg that was black on the bottom and green on the top. You didn't have to be a farm girl to know that egg had gone bad.

We'd get phone calls in the middle of the night too, just enough to disturb our sleep. We were all sure the rooms were bugged, but what purpose that would serve, nobody really knew. It was a weird situation and we certainly weren't treated like special guests in the country.

We did our best to counter that, especially on the food front. Eleanor had the foresight to bring over provisions like peanut butter, granola, chocolate bars, and cookies. We had our own steaks brought over, but the Russian chefs soon wound up selling them, and some of our stash of beer was hijacked too!

None of this did anything to ease the tensions between the two cultures. It's been well documented, but this series was about more than just hockey – it was about our way of life versus theirs. And with every game in this series, those tensions only increased. Thank goodness that we had those three thousand crazy Canadians in the stands in Russia cheering us on – those great fans really lifted our spirits.

Many people have since speculated that it was the Russians' way of trying to throw us off our games, and that might have been part of it. But some of it I think was more about incompetence than anything sinister. There was little to no accountability in the communist system at that time, and I really believe it was more a case of mismanagement than a plot against us. But whatever the case, it wasn't a factor once the games were on. We were ready to play from the moment we got over there and we were intent on winning the series.

It was important for us to keep our sense of humour, given

the conditions in Russia. And we did, although once two of our players took the humour part a little far.

One day during the series, we were at the hotel and, as usual, we weren't looking forward to any of the meals we'd be getting. But some good news came courtesy of Chicago Blackhawks defencemen Bill White and Pat Stapleton, who were well-known jokesters.

White was about six-foot-four and Stapleton was about four-foot-six, so they were a funny pair to start with. But they really sucked us in once by announcing they had found this fantastic Chinese restaurant and made arrangements for the whole team to eat there. We couldn't believe our luck – we had been searching high and low for better food to eat, and here they had discovered a great place.

They went around telling everyone that the buses would pick everybody up in front of the hotel at 6:00 p.m. and we'd all go together and have a terrific dinner. That really lifted the mood – until, of course, we found out that it was that duo's idea of a practical joke and that there was no Chinese restaurant anywhere near the hotel! Groups were even meeting in the lobby to head out together, only to find out it was all a hoax.

The worst part of it all: somebody actually cancelled the team's dinner at the hotel that night in anticipation of the Chinese feast, so we were completely out of luck that night! Ah, but White and Whitey (as Stapleton is known) had the right idea – they wanted to inject some levity into the situation and help us laugh and relax a bit. And you know, it worked . . . after we got over missing dinner, of course!

Despite the hole we were in, I would describe our mood as more expectant than nervous. We basically knew who was going to be playing by this point, so that distraction had been removed, and I was really looking forward to playing in the games over there.

First, things were going quite well for me. Our line was playing very solid hockey at both ends of the rink. Ronnie, Bobby, and I had jelled so that we were certain we'd be in the lineup for every game. I liked the idea of the big ice surface too; I remember telling Eleanor that this larger ice surface was my cup of tea. My strengths had always been my speed and my shot, so I felt this was the perfect scenario for me. I was very, very confident heading into game five.

Then, of course, we experienced international refereeing again. Like I said, there were no excuses, but my goodness, was the officiating ever inconsistent in that fifth game! We had a quiet assurance that we could come back in the series, and to a man we felt that we outplayed the Russians in that fifth game of the series after it was over. And early on, everything looked great.

J.P. Parise opened the scoring late in the first period, I fed Clarke a pass later on and he beat Tretiak to make it 2–0, and I scored at 11:58 to give us a 3–0 advantage. What a great start to the Russian leg of the series!

But it all fell apart for us. I was tripped and went head first into the boards at full speed and had to be helped off the ice. Jim Murray, our doctor, informed me I had a concussion. Against doctor's orders I trudged back out there and scored with fifteen minutes left to play to give us a 4–1 lead after the Russians had gotten on the scoreboard – that second goal came with me suffering from a pounding headache, but nothing was keeping me from being out there!

——

There are so many concussions in hockey these days, and so much written and said about them. It seems that concussions, and their effects on athletes, have become the biggest single worry in hockey, especially since they've happened to some of the game's greatest stars.

I have had six concussions since I started playing hockey, so I certainly know what they feel like and how bad they can be. They have happened at various times in my playing career, including the one I had right in the middle of the Canada–Russia series. I had some at the start of my career and others later on too.

The first one was in my first junior B game – I was knocked out cold in a game against the St. Marys Lincolns while playing for the Goderich Sailors. I also got one in my first game of junior A. My third concussion happened in 1966 in the NHL when I got nailed on the temple by a slap shot from Doug Barkley with the Detroit Red Wings, and that was the concussion that convinced me to put on a helmet and keep it on during my playing career.

After that concussion, the doctors made me play the rest of the year with a helmet, and it took a while to get used to. But eventually I got comfortable wearing it and I kept one on from that point after. Eleanor also really wanted me to keep wearing one and that certainly helped me make my decision.

It was a different era then, to be sure. Most teams didn't want their players wearing helmets, and the Red Wings were one such team. Our coach and general manager, Sid Abel, made that clear to me as soon as I started wearing one the next season. Now, I had worked out a deal with CCM that paid me to wear their helmet on the ice, and when I told Sid what the deal was worth, he was surprised and at least understood my position a little better. But I had to promise him that, if the helmet hurt my ability to play in any way, shape, or form, I'd take it off.

Soon after I started wearing it, I scored four goals in a game against the New York Rangers. Sid saw me after that game and said there would be no problem with me wearing a helmet, and it was never an issue after that. Stan Mikita, one of the best scorers in hockey at the time and a future Hockey Hall of Famer, had put on a helmet the year before, which also helped relieve any stigma.

I guess it was just a sign of the times. Wearing a helmet was looked at as a sign of weakness in some quarters. The thinking was wrong, of course, especially with what we know now about concussions. Just imagine a player not wearing a helmet today. The mere idea is ridiculous. But our knowledge about concussions wasn't what it is today, and if we knew then what we know now, our thinking would have been different – at least I hope so.

Even when I was wearing a helmet, I know I played hurt at times, but you just did back then – that's the way it was. Everybody plays hurt in hockey, even today, but in the six-team era, if you were out of the lineup too long, you ran the risk of losing your job. With so few NHL jobs around, you just couldn't afford to take that chance.

I would play with headaches, pounding headaches. But remember, this was a different era. We wouldn't do that today. The concussion in game five in Moscow was probably the worst-timed of them all. I was examined by Jim Murray, our team doctor, and he was adamant – I had a concussion. He basically told me I was done. I couldn't go back on the ice during the biggest series of my life.

Harry Sinden, our coach, came into the dressing room and conferred with him. The doctor told him in no uncertain terms that I had to sit out, at least for the rest of that game.

"Harry, don't do this to me," I pleaded. "I want to play, I've got to play."

Harry was a good coach and a responsible man, and he didn't want to risk my health any more than the doctor did. But when he saw how adamant I was about getting back into that game and the series, he relented.

"If you really want to play, I'm not going to stop you," Harry said. And I was back out there for the next period – not only for that game, but for the rest of the series.

Now, again, I have to emphasize: this was 1972, when we knew basically nothing about head injuries, and we were in a dressing room in Russia to boot, so there sure wasn't going to be any advanced medical screening. So . . . back on the ice I went. There is no way that I, or any other player, would be let back on the ice under those circumstances today. No way. Does that make my decision wrong? Not in my mind. There was nothing that would keep me out of that series, and since the true dangers of being concussed were not known, I felt then – and still feel now – it was the right thing to do. Fortunately for me, despite the massive pounding headache I had for the rest of the game, I suffered no real long-term effects – at least none that I am aware of! I was lucky, I guess, that none of the six concussions I sustained resulted in any permanent damage. A lot of players have had head injuries that shortened their careers, as we all know. As it is, I can afford to joke about it – I tell everybody I'd be a lot more intelligent than I am today if I hadn't had six concussions and cancer. My illnesses have given me a good excuse for everything!

But all kidding aside, my main point is that it is not hypocritical to think differently about a serious issue in retrospect. Changing your mind isn't a sign of hypocrisy, it's just a sign that maybe you've gotten a little wiser over the years. The great Muhammad Ali once said that the man who sees the world the same at sixty as he did at thirty has wasted thirty years of his life. That is very true.

Despite our gaining a 4–1 advantage, the Russians came right back. They scored two goals eight seconds apart and wound up scoring four straight goals in ten minutes with Vladimir Vikulov notching the game-winner at 14:46 of the third period, breaking in alone and beating Tony Esposito. Tony slammed his stick on the ice in disgust, and we left the ice wondering how we could have let that game get away, a 5–4 loss.

People look back on this now and wonder how we could have bounced back from such a devastating loss. But as bad as that loss was, there were a lot of positives from that game. There were three thousand crazy Canadian fans in the stands cheering us on, for starters, and that warmed our hearts. We had begun to think the country had abandoned us after the debacle in Vancouver, so that was encouraging.

The refereeing wasn't that great once again, but we had managed to take a three-goal lead twice with it, so we knew it was something we could overcome. Alan Eagleson was doing everything he could to look after our needs there, and although the Russians were in control in their own country, Al kept them honest and always had our backs. We never forgot him for that.

Phil Esposito was an incredible leader for us too. Phil had a remarkable NHL career, but in my mind he was never better than he was in that series in 1972. He played a ton, he led by example, he made the big plays, and he really willed us to win. Even the Russians took to calling him "the man with the big heart."

Phil was an outstanding player for us in that series. He scored seven goals in that eight-game series, a fact I think is sometimes overlooked. We had four assistant captains on that team, and he was one of them, but right off the bat it became evident who the real leader on the team was, and that was Esposito.

Phil Esposito in 1972 was, in my mind, the best forward in all of hockey. He was at his best when he was in the slot and so dangerous from in close. He was like a bag of cement out there – you couldn't move him. He had such a great shot, a great release, and every time he was in position and fired the puck, the goalie he was facing had to make a great stop or that puck was going in the net.

Phil was notorious for not working very hard to get into shape – he'll be the first to admit that – but despite that he really had such incredible stamina. I felt I was in a lot better shape than he was, but he could stay out there on a shift way longer than I could, he just had such great stamina and drive. He really was quite a workhorse.

He was a great, great player, but he would have been really scary if he had been in top shape. If I had lived the lifestyle he did, well, I wouldn't have been able to take it! But Phil was larger than life. What really stood out about him on the ice was his presence, he just had a commanding presence, and he could do everything you asked him to do out on the ice. On a good night, he was just about unstoppable, and there were a lot of those nights in his career.

He wasn't a dirty player by any means, but he played hard. He's a big, lovable guy too, and anybody who knows Phil likes him. He really is a terrific guy to be around. There's no way we could have won the 1972 series without him in the lineup. He led us on and off the ice in that series.

Harry Sinden remained the calming influence, even after the loss in the fifth game. He reminded us again of his mantra – "One game at a time, guys; one game at a time" – and that all we had to worry about was winning game six. The other games in the series would look after themselves – and that was reassuring to us.

Yes, we were down 1–3–1 now in the series and faced the daunting prospect of having to win three straight games on enemy ice to win the series, but we still had a sense of confidence, believe it or not. We were getting into shape, and we were becoming a very strong and stable hockey club. We went into game six confident that we could outplay them again and that we could win the next game.

For game six, Ken Dryden took over in goal from Tony Esposito. Rod Seiling and Frank Mahovlich sat out, and Red Berenson, Serge Savard, and Dennis Hull were inserted into the lineup. We had a game plan now; it was just a matter of executing it. And we were still loose, hard as it may be to believe. I remember kidding Dennis Hull – who was being brought back into the lineup – on the bus on the way to the rink, saying, "Come on, Moses, time to lead us out of the wilderness." And you know, Dennis played very well for us and really made a positive impact playing with Jean Ratelle and Rod Gilbert.

It wasn't a spectacular win in game six, but it was still a victory. Hull played Moses to the hilt by scoring the first goal, and Yvan Cournoyer and I also had goals as we held on for a 3–2 win. That was the score after two periods, and that's the way it stayed, as we outshot the Russians 17–7 in the final twenty minutes and Dryden had what was probably his best game of the series.

We were right back in the series and we knew it. So did the Russians. And leave it to Harry to again proclaim, "Just worry about game seven now, and we'll tackle game eight when we get there." His philosophy was working, we were taking one game at a time and not worrying about the game after.

Securing the win in game six was great, of course. My confidence was already sky-high as a result of the way things had gone in Canada during the series, and our line was playing well. We were all contributing, our whole team was rounding into form, and we had a sense we would prevail and win the series.

One of the great things about the 1972 Summit Series was that we became teammates for life. Maybe it is politically incorrect to refer to a hockey series as a war these days, but that's what it felt like to us. Because of the political tensions off the ice and the at-times brutal play on the ice, it was more like war than hockey in the minds of us players.

When you go to war with someone, you share a common bond forever, and as a result, all of us who were on Team Canada '72 remain close after all these years. What got us through that series was our spirit and our common belief that we were representing our country and that we would all do anything it took to win that series.

Anything.

Of the thirty-five players on that roster, nobody was more of a competitor than Bobby Clarke when it came to doing whatever it took to win. If this was really a war, Clarke was the ultimate warrior, the one guy who took no prisoners, would never surrender, would battle until the bitter end.

He was a great teammate, and we all knew that. I respected him then, and I respect him now, for all he brought to the table and to our team. It's now forty years since that memorable series and I haven't changed my view of Bobby Clarke one bit in all that time.

But I have changed my view of The Slash – which is still talked about almost as much as my winning goal in game eight.

We had struggled against the Russians enormously in the series, right from the get-go. By the time we got to the Soviet Union for the final four games of the series, we knew first-hand just how tough this Russian team was to handle on the ice.

One player in particular, the great Valeri Kharlamov, was causing us fits. It was clear by the time we got to Russia that he was a player we were going to have to find a way to stop if we were going to win the series. And in game six, Clarke found a way to stop him: a vicious slash to his ankle. There can be no doubt that he intended to knock the Russian great out of the game. That's just the way Bobby played hockey.

I didn't see the slash when it happened, but I wasn't that upset with it. We were all caught up in the moment. Today, a slash like that would result in an automatic suspension, that's for sure. Could you imagine, say, the Detroit Red Wings going out and deliberately breaking Sidney Crosby's ankle so they could have a better chance of winning the Stanley Cup? But, as was the case with concussions, it was a different era and there was a different philosophy. We all supported Bobby; we all wanted to win that much.

As I mentioned, as the years have gone by, we have remained close teammates, all of us, getting together whenever possible for special events such as anniversary celebrations. In 2002, I was at a hockey game when a reporter asked me what I thought, with the benefit of thirty years of hindsight, of the slash that led to Kharlamov's ankle being broken. I should have been more wary of the question.

"It was the low point of the series," I said, and my comments were broadcast widely by the media.

They obviously hurt Bobby a great deal. "I think it's improper to criticize a teammate thirty years later," he responded in the *Globe and Mail*. "If it was so offensive, why didn't he bother to say something after the game?

"I'm surprised at him, because we were a true team. Thirty years ago, we put forth the ultimate team performance. I thought it was foolish for him to say that. It doesn't hurt me, but I don't understand why he would bring it up now."

I regret that Bobby was upset by my remarks and I apologized to him profusely afterwards. But I want to take this opportunity to set the record straight on exactly how I feel on this issue.

I now feel the reporter was just looking to create some controversy and get himself a story, and he sure did. First of all, I didn't bring the subject up. I was blindsided by his question, and all I said was that I thought it was wrong in terms of my grandchildren, who were now playing hockey. He conveniently left that point out.

I told him I would hate the thought of a coach telling a player to break the ankle of one of my grandchildren in a hockey game, for instance, or having my grandchildren doing the slashing. I answered the question in that light, and I answered it honestly. In terms of sportsmanship, I have always felt that if you can't beat them straight up, you don't deserve to win. Yes, emotions were stirred up in 1972, and in the heat of the moment it seems like anything goes. But when you get more rational, you have to realize that the end doesn't justify the means.

I didn't condemn Bobby Clarke in 1972, but I'm a very different person today than I was then. Many of us are.

I feel similarly about the concussion issue – does it make sense to think and feel the same way about concussions now as we did back then? Should we still think and feel the same way about breaking a player's ankle in the heat of the moment in a hockey game as we did in 1972?

Changing your viewpoint on any issue when you have new information, or when you have become more enlightened in your life, doesn't make you a hypocrite; it makes you a wiser person. If we cannot learn in retrospect about our behaviour after four decades, will we ever learn?

I feel the same way about Bobby Clarke's slash as I do about my decision to go back onto the ice with a concussion when the doctor told me not to.

At the time, both seemed to be the right thing to do. With the benefit of wisdom gained over the years, in retrospect, they were wrong. I ask myself the question: would I want my grandchildren to do what Bobby Clarke or I did in 1972? The answer is no, I wouldn't.

If we cannot learn from our past, then we really have wasted years of our lives. I am very sorry I hurt Bobby Clarke with my comments, but the real point of what happened around that particular story is that I should have been more careful when answering a loaded question from a reporter I didn't know very well, and now have little respect for.

This is one of the many reasons players today are very wary around certain writers.

For game seven, Sinden decided to put Tony Esposito in goal and inserted Bill Goldsworthy in place of Red Berenson. This one was a tense back-and-forth battle that came right down to the wire.

Espo opened the scoring, taking passes from Ellis and me to beat Tretiak just as a power play was coming to an end. Alexander Yakushev got one back for the Russians before Vladimir Petrov deked out Tony Esposito to give the Russians a 2–1 edge. Serge Savard then made a great spinarama move and fed Espo in the slot, who again fired a shot home, leaving the score tied 2–2 after the first period.

The second period was scoreless before Rod Gilbert gave us the lead early in the third period, but another goal by Yakushev on yet another Russian power play tied the game. Time was winding down in the third period with the score tied 3–3, and even though we felt we were outplaying the Russians again, we appeared headed for the second tie game of the series.

That, of course, would do us no good whatsoever. Russia would still lead the series 3–2–2 with another tie, which meant the best we could hope for was a tie in the series if we happened to win game eight. I really felt we were going to have to pull the goalie if it came down to the final minute or so, as a tie in this game would accomplish nothing for us.

With three minutes to go in the game, I got what would likely be my last shift of the night. I know it may be hard to believe, but things were going so well for me at that point that I really believed I was going to score.

Savard hit me with a pass at centre ice, and after dodging one of their forwards, I came to the blue line alone. Two defencemen greeted me, and the one to my left tried to swipe the puck away just as I was trying to slip the puck through his legs. The puck hit his skate and I was able to pick it up again and keep on going, with the defenceman on my right now moving over to try to take me out.

He wound up tripping me, but I was able keep the puck in front of me and my stick away from him. As I was going down, Tretiak dropped to his knees, anticipating a low shot since I was falling, but I managed to rifle a shot over his right shoulder just under the crossbar for the game-winning goal.

What a moment! Without question that was one of the most satisfying goals I had ever scored in my life, and certainly the best one from my point of view. It was a crucial one, and the players came off the bench to mob me behind the net as it gave us a 4–3 lead with just two minutes remaining in that pivotal game seven.

We killed off the final minutes and had come all the way back to even the series at 3–3–1 with that 4–3 victory. I had scored the game-winning goals in games six and seven, and now it would all come down to an eighth and deciding game.

It was an incredible thrill, and we celebrated in the dressing room because, despite everything we had been through, we could still win this series. I was still on cloud nine as we went back to the hotel to rest up for the final game two days later.

To this day, I can remember telling Eleanor, "Honey, I'll probably never score a bigger goal in my life."

Well, as we all know now, I had one more big goal left in me.

CHAPTER SEVEN

THURSDAY, SEPTEMBER 28, 1972. THE BIGGEST DAY in Canadian hockey history up to that point, perhaps, and in retrospect it may still be. I will leave that up to the hockey historians to decide; all I know is that it was a momentous day for our team, for the three thousand Canadian fans in the stands, and for the millions of Canadians watching across the country anywhere there was a television set.

But it didn't start out very well.

Emotionally, we were sky high heading into that eighth game, and looking back on it, that almost cost us in the same way as our hyper feelings did before game one – but this time, just early.

We got into trouble by taking two holding penalties and faced a five-on-three. You can't do that against the Russians, and Yakushev made us pay, knocking a rebound past Dryden to open the scoring. We got our own power play a little later, and Sinden started using Ron Ellis and me with Espo on the power play. We were out there with him when a

Russian defenceman did us a big favour by knocking in a rebound from Brad Park's shot into his own goal to tie the score. The goal was credited to Phil, who was right there, but he never actually touched the puck – anyway, the score was now tied 1–1.

· Then once again, the questionable officiating we had seen all series reared its ugly head. Much has been said in previous accounts of the series on the work of referee Josef Kompalla, and I've resisted bringing him up until now. He called a penalty from the other side of the ice on J.P. Parise for interference and J.P. was so incensed he swung his stick at the West German referee. Naturally he was tossed out of the game, sending the players and coaches and Canadian fans in the stands into a frenzy.

The frustrations had reached the boiling point by then. Some of our fans were even chanting, "Let's go home!" And to be perfectly honest, I turned to Ron Ellis on the bench and said, "Let's get out of here." If Harry Sinden had told us to leave we would have, that's how much of a joke the officiating was. But really, there was nowhere to go; we had come so far that we had to see this through to the brutal end.

Another Russian power-play goal put them ahead 2–1, but we again tied the score at 2–2 when Jean Ratelle set up Brad Park on a neat passing play.

Vladimir Shadrin scored twenty-one seconds into the period, but Bill White scored at 10:32 to again tie the score at 3–3. This game was going back and forth, and despite our desire to win, we were really in a battle once again, and we knew it.

The Russians were determined to win this game too, and they scored twice more before the period ended, as Yakushev beat Dryden at 11:43 and Shadrin tallied on yet another power play at 16:44. We were down 5–3 after two periods, and things certainly looked bleak.

During the intermission, we knew we couldn't gamble too much too soon. But down by two goals now, we knew we needed to score. We had just twenty minutes left, so we came out with lots of energy and anticipation that we could make something happen in time. Our leader, Phil Esposito, scored off a great pass from Peter Mahovlich to get us right back into the game. The Russians started playing a little too defensively and we kept coming, and at 12:56 Yvan Cournoyer tied the game by swatting a rebound off a shot by Esposito past Tretiak.

When the goal light didn't come on to signal the goal, Alan Eagleson went crazy in the stands. He felt that the Russians were up to no good again, and he wanted the goal judge removed. The Russian soldiers grabbed Eagleson and were taking him away when Peter Mahovlich jumped over the boards and rescued him from the soldiers. Those who witnessed it will know just how high emotions were running at that point. It really was a spectacle.

But there was still work to do. The game was tied 5–5 and the series was tied 3–3–1. The Russians had outscored us 32–30, and they informed us at our bench that if this game ended in a tie, they would be claiming victory because they had scored more goals than we had in the series. We knew that we had to win the game in order to win the series.

Time ticked down. There was less than a minute to play at Luzhniki Arena and the fans were on the edge of their seats. Esposito, Cournoyer, and Peter Mahovlich were on the ice in that final minute as I watched from the bench. I then did something I had never done before, and would never do again in my hockey career.

"Pete! Pete!" I hollered at him. Don't ask me how or why, but I felt if I could get out there one more time I could score a goal. I just felt it. For the first time in my life I was screaming at a player to get off the ice so I could get on, just one more time. You just didn't do that – I had never heard another player do it in my eighteen-year hockey career – but I did.

"Pete! Pete!" I hollered for a second time and then a third. Finally, Mahovlich skated over to the bench, allowing me to hop over the boards and join the play.

As I got onto the ice, the puck went to Cournoyer on the far boards. I charged to the net and yelled for a pass, but when it came I had to reach forward for it and their defenceman tripped me, my momentum making me fall and slide into the boards behind the Russian goal.

I remember thinking that I still had time to get the puck back again and score. The Russians tried to clear the zone, but Esposito was able to whack the puck toward Tretiak, who made the save. I was on my feet again and alone at the side of the goal, and when Tretiak couldn't control the rebound off Esposito's shot, I tried sliding a shot along the ice, but he blocked it.

The puck came right back to me. With Tretiak now down, I had some room, and I put the puck in the back of the net, with thirty-four seconds left on the clock. And then . . . well, perhaps the best way to describe the whole few moments was the way Foster Hewitt did to millions of Canadians watching at home on television.

"Here's a shot! Henderson made a wild stab at it and fell.

Here's another shot, right in front. They score! Henderson has scored for Canada!"

I have been asked a million times what went through my mind when that puck slid into the goal. I have answered it a million times, but I will tell you one more time now what I even said to myself out loud when that puck went in the net.

"Dad would have loved that one," I said. I even had a sense of melancholy for a nanosecond that he wasn't there to share the moment with me, as he had died in 1968. He was the most influential person in my life when it came to hockey, and at the greatest moment of my hockey life, I wanted to share it with him. After all those years, I guess I was still trying to please my father.

That moment of sadness lasted just a second, though, and was replaced by absolute jubilation! I jumped into Cournoyer's arms, the guys came pouring off the bench, and the celebration was on. My goodness, what a moment in time that was; I still get tingles thinking about it forty years later.

RON ELLIS ON THE GOAL OF THE CENTURY

Our line came off the ice with about two minutes left in the game, I guess, and the score was tied 5–5. We just get back to the bench and Harry Sinden says to us, "Get ready. You're going right back out there." We had the hot hand as a line, but that was still pretty interesting with the team we had, he was going right back to us. So there we are, on the bench, and I'm just trying to get my wind back.

Now Yvan Cournoyer, the guy I would be replacing, is on the other side of the ice and I'm watching him. With around a minute left in the game, I am sitting right beside Paul on the bench. He stands up and starts calling Pete Mahovlich off the ice. I mean, he's yelling at him to get off the ice so he can get on. Professional hockey players just don't do that usually, but Paul really wanted out there.

There's no way I'm getting on for Cournoyer because he's at the other end of the ice, but Mahovlich is a lot closer to the bench. I see Pete's reaction, he hesitates for a second, but Pete comes off the ice. Maybe he had a feeling that Paul could do it again, as he had scored the game-winning goals in both games six and seven, of course.

That's when I played my part in all this: I stepped aside so Paul Henderson could get on the ice!

The funny thing is, if Pete was on the other side of the ice and didn't hear Paul calling, it wouldn't have happened the way it did. It's funny how that worked out. Ten seconds later, the puck goes right into the net as Paul scored the goal. And the rest, well, you've seen it on the clips.

I went back to the bench exhausted. I said, "Harry, I'm done, the tank is empty!" There was no way I was going back out there for the final thirty-four seconds. We killed those seconds off, the clock wound down, and we had the greatest victory of our lives. We were desperate to win and it showed, and that was the difference really. We didn't want to go down in history as the team that couldn't lose to the Russians but did . . . and thanks to that third-period rally, we didn't!

I wound up the series with seven goals and three assists in eight games, third in scoring behind only Phil Esposito (seven goals and six assists) and Alexander Yakushev (seven goals and four assists). I scored the game-winning goals in games six, seven, and eight, all of which were must-wins for Team Canada.

I had been a streak scorer throughout my career, and I had scored some important goals, especially when I was on a hot streak. Once I got on a roll, I tended to stay that way, and that's just the way it was. I did score thirty-eight goals the year prior in the NHL after all, and I was always the kind of guy who, if you surrounded me with good players who'd get me the puck, could score goals.

That said, of course, that eight-game series was the ultimate high of my career. Harry Sinden said in his book that I never had a bad game, never even had a bad shift in that series. That was very kind of him. I played my best hockey at the time when it mattered the most: when I was representing my country in such an important series. I take great satisfaction in that.

After the game, we went back to the dressing room and I sipped on a beer, absolutely spent after the emotion of it all. I looked around and realized that there wasn't a single person in that room who didn't make a significant contribution to what we had accomplished. Players like Gary Bergman, who never got the credit he deserved for being such a terrific stay-at-home defenceman in the NHL with Detroit, played brilliantly beside Brad Park, a true Hall of Famer. Esposito was unreal, of course – he was the true leader. Clarke was simply amazing. His enthusiasm and work ethic were contagious. Ron Ellis, the consummate defensive specialist, had a great series despite the fact he was hurting badly throughout it with a neck injury. Even though Ron was less than 100 percent, there were no Russians who wanted any part of him checking them, and I feel we wouldn't have won the series without Ron's great defensive work. Tony Esposito played so well at times in the series, and Ken Dryden didn't allow a goal under enormous pressure in the third period of the final game, and even Brian Glennie, who didn't play a game, stayed with us and was the ultimate cheerleader. In their own ways every single person led us to that win. That was one area where the Russians just could not match us – our intense desire to win and our heart. They were great players, but we had the intangibles going for us that they just didn't have.

What a wonderful experience the series turned out to be for every player who was involved with Team Canada. I will never forget a single moment of it, and I am sure the millions of Canadians who witnessed it will not forget it either. It truly was a great moment in the history of Canadian sport.

After the series ended, I attended a reception for the players on both teams. All of us Canadians attended, but only a handful of Russian players bothered to show up. One of them was their great goaltender, Vladislav Tretiak, who had played tremendously against us.

I went up to him and said through an interpreter that I was really impressed with the way he played through the entire series. He responded, also via interpreter, by telling me I was lucky to have scored the last goal of the series! My response to him was pretty direct – and let's just say no interpreter was needed to translate. He knew exactly what I thought of his response.

Thank goodness we have been able to get to know the Russians since that series ended. I think I can speak for everybody on Team Canada when I say that once we got to know them, we found them to be terrific individuals. The oppressive system that they had to live under and endure as athletes in Russia was very difficult on them, and I now admire them for how well they handled themselves under those circumstances. Once we got to know and understand them better, the dislike we had for them softened considerably.

Vladislav has been a part of some of our get-togethers over the years, and I have gotten to know him quite well while attending several different events and making appearances together. Let me say this about him now: he is a classy guy, a consummate gentleman, and I'm a big fan of his. I am so glad I got the opportunity to know him better.

We had to make a brief stopover in Czechoslovakia to play a game against the Czechs, which was anticlimactic at that point. I asked Harry if I could sit this one out since I had really aggravated my groin injury against the Russians, and he said okay. All I remember about that trip was that they had such fine crystal in Czechoslovakia then, and Eleanor made sure I purchased some for us as the gals didn't get to go to Prague. I did, and we returned home exhausted but happy with what we had accomplished.

What I didn't know – and what none of us knew – was what was waiting for us when we finally did get back home.

CHAPTER EIGHT

I HAVE BEEN INVOLVED WITH A WEBSITE CALLED 72project.com – run by Sean Mitton, the founder of the Canadian Expat Network – where Canadians of all ages can share their remembrances of the 1972 Canada–Russia series with a younger generation of hockey fans.

I think the website offers a great way for Canadians to participate in the fortieth anniversary celebrations, and it is really humbling to see how our victory, and the final goal in particular, affected so many Canadians watching at home. I encourage you to check it out. There is a lot of great stuff there, including stories from people from all walks of life and some famous Canadians as well.

I'd also like to share with you here just a few of these stories from some prominent Canadians as to where they were during the eighth and final game, and their memories.

GLENN HOWARD, three-time world champion curler

I was ten and my brother Russ (an Olympic gold medallist in curling in 2006) was seventeen during the '72 series. I was a typical Canadian kid who was passionate about hockey. Before the series started, we felt that Canada would show them whose game it was. But it was surreal how good the Russians were.

The fans were really hard on the players, and I remember Espo's speech after one of the games. The team showed its grit and Canadian pride. The Russians may have been in better shape, but our guys dug deep.

For Russ and me, Paul Henderson was our favourite player because we liked guys who skated fast. So his success in the series had us bouncing off the walls. I watched the final game with all my buddies in the gym at Parkview School in Midland, Ontario, and went crazy when Henderson scored. I get goose bumps thinking about it.

JIM CUDDY, co-founder of Blue Rodeo

I was a Toronto Maple Leafs fan and [band co-founder] Greg [Keelor] liked the Canadiens. The guys I cheered for included Frank Mahovlich, Davey Keon, and Carl Brewer. The day of the eighth and final game, the school let everyone go home early. So we went to my friend Donald Wilkin's house for a party to watch the game. There may have been between fifty and seventy people, including Greg. We all celebrated when Henderson scored!

GREG KEELOR, co-founder of Blue Rodeo

In 1972, I was trying out as a goalie for the Toronto Marlies and we practised at the historic Maple Leaf Gardens. At the end of the tryout, I was the last guy on the ice, and Team Canada '72 would be the next team to practise. At the end of the rink, Bobby Orr steps on the ice. He was injured and didn't play in the series but was on the roster. Orr's out there, kind of goofing around and taking shots on me. A few minutes later, [former] Toronto Maple Leafs great Frank Mahovlich joins in. We played for about thirty minutes.

Carolina Hurricanes trainer PETER FRIESEN

Midway through the series, Phil Esposito's talk captivated me. He spoke to the effect that all the cards were stacked against Team Canada after the tough start. He was one of the guys who got the nation to support Team Canada. It was a showcase event that grabbed the whole country.

During the final game, I was in the ninth grade at Prince Albert Collegiate Institute. I recall the game was around midday, and the teacher wheeled the TV into a packed classroom. The black-and-white reception wasn't great, it wasn't anything like today's HDTVs. When Henderson scored, we definitely jumped up and down. It made everyone so proud to be a Canadian and to appreciate how great the sport of hockey is.

It's always kind of neat to read about the experiences of well-known Canadians, but some of the best stories I have heard have come from ordinary Canadians. It's really humbling to me to learn how many Canadians from so many different walks of life were touched by what we accomplished in Moscow, and I am very thankful to have been a part of such an important and historic moment in Canadian history.

Ever since the day we returned from Moscow, people have approached me to tell me where they were and what they were doing when I scored The Goal on September 28, 1972.

Some of the stories really stand out in my mind, and some of them listed below I wrote about years ago in *Shooting for Glory*. The Goal actually changed some people's lives, believe it or not, and these stories never get old to me.

For instance, I received a letter from one woman who started out by telling me I owed her some money because of The Goal. That was a first.

She and her husband had just moved into a new home the day of the final game. She was unpacking some dishes and setting them down on a table while the game played on the television in another room. As the seconds wound down, she was busy unpacking and had a dish in each hand.

She heard Foster Hewitt's famous call of the goal and lost her composure with joy. Without thinking, she threw the dishes in the air, sending the fine china to the ceiling. The dishes hit the ceiling and fell back to the floor, shattering into pieces!

Her letter said that the goal provided her with one of the greatest thrills of her life – after she got over the fact that it had also cost her some pretty fine china. I would like to sincerely apologize to her for her loss, but I'm sorry to say I do not owe her any money as a result!

That woman wasn't the only person to write me and suggest they should be compensated. A gentleman in Ontario told me that he and two of his buddies were out fishing the day of the final game and were listening to it on the radio. When the goal was scored, he jumped up and was so excited that he went overboard into the water! As he went over the side, he knocked his tackle box into the water as well.

His buddies saved him and pulled him back into the boat, but the tackle box sank to the bottom, filled with his fishing gear. This guy told me that since I was responsible for scoring the game-winning goal, it would be a good idea if I were also to help him replace his equipment. Sorry, my friend. I may have caused you to fall, but I'm not liable!

Numerous times over the years, people have shown me evidence of damage inflicted on their property after The Goal was scored. I've heard lots of tales of how chairs and desks and even chandeliers were dented as a result of somebody throwing something. One guy even showed me his desk, which had a big gouge in it, and explained why he left it the way it was.

"When you scored the goal, I threw my chair back and it smashed the desk," he said. "I won't fix it because it will always remind me of the goal."

Another guy broke a chair when I scored and he kept it in his recreation room as a permanent memento of the occasion. Over the years, I've seen beer stains on walls from people tossing their beer, and they point to the exact spot as if it's a shrine.

Before I get to some of the stranger and funnier stories I've been told over the years, I'd like to share with you one that came from a woman in Toronto who claimed that The Goal saved her marriage.

In her moving letter to me, she wrote that she had recently separated from her husband and they had decided to get a divorce. On the day game eight was played, the husband came over to the house to get her to sign the divorce papers.

The third period was just about to start as he arrived, and he noticed it was on the TV, so he asked her if he could stay and watch. She agreed, but they sat there in silence and watched the events unfold. When I scored the goal, they jumped up and started dancing, and hugged each other in celebration.

The woman said they looked into each other's eyes and realized that they still loved each other. It was an emotional moment for both of them, but not just because they were happy Canada won. Sharing such a special moment together gave them a new perspective, and they decided to get back together and give their marriage another try.

I received her letter around Christmas 1972, three months after The Goal was scored. She thanked me for the best Christmas present she could have ever imagined. She said that I had provided them with one more opportunity to spend some time together, and as a result, they had reconciled and were back together.

If I hadn't scored, she said, her husband might have left without even looking at her again. Of all the things that goal did, that might have been the best one.

I had just finished speaking at a church one day when I was approached by two grizzled farmers who wanted to tell me their story.

They were on a farm just north of Toronto and were listening to the game on the radio while they worked on a silo. When The Goal went in, they grabbed each other and started dancing around, filled with joy. They couldn't contain themselves. They just shouted with glee and danced around like they were kids. The farmer who told me the story laughed so hard at the memory that he had tears in his eyes, even though it was years later.

"I'm so glad nobody saw us dancing like two old fools," he told me. "They would have locked us up for good."

I must admit I get a little teary myself hearing simple, wonderful stories like that.

I heard another story regarding farm life and The Goal that I got a real kick out of. In Listowel, Ontario, they used to have an annual plowing match. Well, on September 28, 1972, it was time for the annual event. Many people in attendance brought along their radios to listen to game eight, of course, as nobody wanted to miss the game, even for a local tradition.

The key to success in a plowing event is to maintain a straight line and plow the rows in an orderly fashion. One farmer set out to do his thing with a radio on top of his tractor so he could hear the game at the same time.

He was maybe three-quarters of the way down the field, I was told, when I scored the goal. He was so excited, he jumped onto the hood of the tractor and started dancing – while it was still running! His exuberance cost him in the competition – his tractor had swerved all over the place and ruined all his rows.

I guess he lost the match – but at least he was happy that he got to hear a piece of history while he was driving!

———

There were American visitors in the country at the time The Goal was scored, of course, and they may have had a little trouble understanding what the big deal was, especially in the middle of the day.

I heard a great story about what happened to an American guest speaker at a teachers' convention in Toronto while the final game was being played. Although the delegation was quiet while he spoke, unbeknownst to him, he didn't have their full attention, as many people in the audience were listening to the game on their transistor radios. When Yvan Cournoyer scored his goal to tie the game at 5–5, a murmur came from the audience, causing the speaker to be startled for a moment. But he continued undaunted.

When I scored, however, the place went crazy. He had no idea what had happened as the hall erupted in cheers and a celebration broke out. Somebody was finally good enough to inform him what had happened, and told him the importance of the goal. I hope he wasn't offended – Canadians are usually much more polite to American visitors!

It's amazing how many people actually heard the game on the radio instead of watching it on television. As many of the stories I've heard demonstrate, not everybody could make it front of a television in the middle of the day – especially in the Northwest Territories.

I was told about three men who were travelling in a car in a very remote part of the Northwest Territories. Their radio reception was fading as they made their way through terrain marked by peaks and valleys. With about five minutes to play in the game, they finally had a decent signal, so they decided to pull over and listen. It wasn't the kind of place where you pulled over unless you had a serious problem, but they didn't want to risk missing any of the final few minutes.

In the freezing cold, they stopped and listened. When I scored the goal, I was told, they jumped out of the car and ran around yelling, "We won! We won!"

Another car approached and, naturally, the driver was concerned at the site of anyone pulled over in the middle of nowhere. The would-be good Samaritan had no idea what had happened, but after being informed about why the other travellers were out there, their smiles were enough to warm up even the coldest place on earth.

A disc jockey from a Toronto radio station told me he was on the air at the time The Goal was scored. He went a little crazy, as he was a passionate Canadian hockey fan. But that wasn't the end of it. The next night, he was DJing at a dance, and about halfway through the event, he decided to play "O Canada!" in honour of Team Canada's victory. He told me the emotions were still so raw that there wasn't a dry eye in the house as people sang along to our national anthem.

The DJ told me he was blubbering by the time it was done, well over a day after it happened. Those stories really do make me proud to be a Canadian.

Life did go on despite the game being played on a Thursday afternoon. While a large part of the country put everything aside to watch the game on TV or listen to it on the radio, flights certainly didn't get cancelled.

This story comes from some people who were on a Canadian airliner during the final game. The pilot was providing updates for the passengers throughout the flight, and first informed them over the PA that the score was 5–3 for Russia after two periods. The next update was 5–4. Then Canada had tied the game at 5–5. And then, of course, the final update after the game was over: Canada had won 6–5! I'm told the passengers and crew spontaneously broke out into "O Canada!" The crew was in such a great mood that they gave passengers free drinks to celebrate!

Hmm . . . maybe when it's all said and done, *I'm* the guy who's owed something!

Because of the timing of the game, a lot of people were in school when it was broadcast, both teachers and students. In his introduction, my co-author, Roger Lajoie, told of being in school when The Goal was scored, and I've heard many stories from people who experienced game eight in their schools too.

One man from Toronto, however, never forgave his teacher for not letting him watch the game. While many schools let their students watch the game together, his teacher wasn't buying in.

"Our teacher made us stay in class and we didn't get to see the game," he told me. "I've hated that teacher ever since."

I could see while listening to his story that this man's animosity toward his teacher was genuine, even decades later! To all the teachers who *did* let students watch the game, I say thanks.

Another man told me how he and his fellow students in law school at Queen's University watched the game despite the fact they had the bar exam the next day. They were supposed to be studying to make their final preparations for what might be the most important test of their lives, and instead they watched the game!

"We had to watch it," he told me. "There was no way we were going to miss it."

It took them several hours to come down from the high after Canada's victory – but they managed finally to hit the books. They studied all night and passed their exams the next day. I hope that Team Canada's win inspired them.

I tell the story of how I called Peter Mahovlich off the ice moments before I scored the game-winning goal in game eight. I somehow had the feeling I would score that goal if I got the chance – and apparently I was not alone in my belief.

A doctor from Oakville, Ontario, told me his story. He was working at a clinic in Mississauga the day of the final game and was giving the patients he saw that day some really fast medical care – because he was running next door to catch some of the game on a small black-and-white TV in a pharmacy in between patients! When there was about five minutes to play and the score was tied 5–5, he'd had enough of the running back and forth. He told his receptionist, "I'm not seeing anybody else until the game's over. You'll have to tell them to wait."

He rushed back to the pharmacy, where a crowd had now gathered for the last moments of the series. Throughout the country, just about everything came to a stop at that point. He told me that the crowd in the pharmacy started to chant, "We want Henderson! We want Henderson!"

When I jumped onto the ice and scored the goal in the final minute, they yelled, "We told you! We told you!"

Looks like I wasn't the only person with a premonition about The Goal.

———

As I have said in this book, I did not become a Christian until a few years after the 1972 series. However, there were apparently some good Christians out there praying for me on that Thursday afternoon.

I've had maybe five different women tell me they actually prayed that I would score the winning goal – and strangely enough, no man has ever told me that. I appreciate the kind thought, and I guess they were praying it would be me because I had already scored the game winners in games six and seven.

I wouldn't pray for something like that now that I am a Christian. I only ask the Lord to help me give it my best, and that His will is done, but the fact that people cared enough to try to get some divine help is touching.

One Catholic lady told me she promised the Lord she would go to church every day for a month if I scored. She tried to live up to the promise but admitted she couldn't and hoped that the Lord would understand. Another woman told me she wasn't really a hockey fan, but she was completely riveted to the last three games in Moscow. She told me she also found herself praying for me in the final game, which was unusual for her, and thanking God when I scored.

All kids like to pretend they are big NHL stars when they are playing road hockey. Before September 28, 1972, I don't imagine too many kids were calling dibs on being Paul Henderson. But one mother told me a story about her son playing road hockey just after I scored the goal. The neighbourhood kids were so excited they just had to get out on the road and play some ball hockey. She told me that all the boys wanted to be Paul Henderson.

"I'm Paul Henderson! I'm Paul Henderson!" they cried. The mother of this little hockey player had to go out and try to settle the dispute. Later on, this same young fellow made his mom get him a Paul Henderson helmet, as no other helmet would do.

The Goal certainly did a lot for my being "drafted" in road hockey games, and it certainly didn't hurt the endorsement deal I had for CCM helmets at the time either!

That story of a marriage saved by The Goal brings to mind another story about a family reunited on the afternoon of game eight of the series.

A woman told me about the troubles her family was having around that time. Her husband and son had a terrible relationship, and the son, who was then fourteen, had stopped talking to his father several months prior.

The final game was on, and mostly by accident the father and son wound up watching the game together. When the goal went in, they jumped to their feet and cheered and, in their exuberance, hugged each other. That simple contact in a moment of joy seemed to break down the walls they had built around each other.

Their excitement continued, and they sat down to dinner together and discussed everything with an open mind. It was the beginning of the healing process for them.

"You absolutely changed the whole atmosphere in my family," the woman told me. "I was caught in the middle between those two. I'll be eternally grateful."

As I will be, for having been the guy who scored the goal that could do that for them.

CHAPTER NINE

We came back from the Summit Series to a tremendous countrywide reaction. We knew the series had captured the imagination of hockey fans across Canada, but we still had no idea how much.

Team Canada first landed in Montreal, where Prime Minister Pierre Trudeau and Montreal mayor Jean Drapeau were among the fans to greet us. The crowd on hand was massive, and they went crazy when we circled the tarmac in fire engines to give them all a closer look. Talk about a terrific homecoming!

From there we went to Nathan Phillips Square in Toronto, where a crowd of maybe fifty thousand fans or so greeted us. It was totally amazing the way the crowds saluted and cheered us, and their outpouring of emotion for the team during a driving fall rain was spine-tingling. As I was introduced, Alan Eagleson and Tony Esposito lifted me onto their shoulders, and it was a moment I will never forget.

It had been an exhausting, exhilarating, and frustrating month all at the same time. We had been booed and vilified at times, but at the end of the day we were treated like heroes wherever we went because we had managed to win the last three games of the series.

I had never experienced anything like that reaction. Playing for the Maple Leafs, I was used to getting a fair amount of fan mail and public recognition, but I was now bombarded with both. I had to hire a secretary to help me with the mail, and I did countless media interviews and appearances, along with being besieged by autograph seekers wherever I went.

I got a lot of promotional offers to capitalize on this sudden fame, and I took advantage of some of them, but frankly some of them were just crazy. I hired Sports Management Inc., a company run by former Maple Leafs trainer Bob Haggert, to look after all my promotional deals. I did a few commercials and some sponsorships, and made some speeches and appearances that were lucrative. I did some work for companies like CCM, Rivera Sports, Granada TV, and Shoppers Drug Mart, but I didn't go overboard – I had seen what excessive greed had done to people in the past, so I was quite content to only do the things I was comfortable in doing.

This was when I first started hearing the stories of how much The Goal meant to other people, of course, and where people were when it was scored. It became one of those "where were you when" kind of moments, and it was quite a thrill to realize that something you had done had turned out to be such an important moment in so many people's lives. And forty years later, it hasn't stopped.

It was a crazy time for me, of course, but my family helped me stay grounded. Eleanor was very happy with my success and new-found fame, and my daughters were mostly good about it too. Our eldest girl, Heather, who was nine at the time, even revelled in our fame! She would line up her friends to meet me and hand out pictures, saying, "Paul Henderson is my dad" to everyone waiting. Jennifer was seven and she was quieter and didn't take kindly to our family life being trampled. She even told a reporter, "I wish my dad was a garbage collector." Jill was just two, so she was oblivious to everything that was going on, except that even she realized her dad was getting a lot of attention suddenly.

Everyone in Canada has a story about where they were when I scored The Goal in Moscow, but the one that is the closest to me involves Heather and Jennifer. Like many children who were in school that day, they watched the final game with their classmates. They both went to the same school, and when the goal was scored, Heather was sitting on a table, watching. Her overexcited classmates charged at her and knocked her to the floor, mobbing her until a friend was able to rescue her. The entire school was dismissed early because the celebration had gotten so out of control.

Heather then went to find Jennifer so that she could take her home, where our third daughter, Jill, was. As I mentioned, Wendy and Darryl Sittler had moved into our house while we were in Moscow to look after the girls, and eventually Heather and Jennifer made it home, trailed by a pack of celebrating classmates.

People started coming to the house to look for autographs and to congratulate the family, and so many of them came that the kids finally had to put up a sign that said, "WE HAVE NO AUTOGRAPHS LEFT" and take the phone off the hook! I can tell you that somebody who was really happy when we got home from Moscow was Wendy Sittler, because she was running our household for us until we returned.

My family was very happy for me, obviously, especially my mother. But her love for me and my siblings didn't have anything to do with how successful we were. She loved all five of her children equally and was always there for us no matter what we did.

My immediate family was then, and still is today, my rock. Without them I couldn't have handled all the demands and pressures associated with having scored such a momentous goal in Canadian hockey history.

I really was sitting on top of the world, but there was still a sense that something was missing in my life, and it wasn't until I examined the spiritual dimension of my life and became a Christian in 1975 that I truly found some peace in my life.

Meanwhile, there was still an NHL career to deal with and to get back to. Somehow I had to put all the distractions that were coming at me behind me and concentrate on returning to the Toronto Maple Leafs for another season, and once again having to play against the great teammates I'd had on Team Canada. The letdown was tremendous.

That next season, 1972–73, was probably the worst of my NHL career for a lot of reasons. First, I played in just forty games because of the groin injury I sustained during the Summit Series, though when I was in the lineup I was productive, scoring eighteen goals and assisting on sixteen more. What made things doubly frustrating was that the Leafs clearly were going nowhere. By 1972, the World Hockey Association had come along, attracting stars and role players alike with some incredible contract offers. Toronto lost Rick Ley, Brad Selwood, Guy Trottier, and Jim Harrison, as well as goaltender Bernie Parent. No coincidence, then, that we went from sixth in the league in goals against to thirteenth. We finished fifth in the East Division that year with just sixty-four points, out of the playoffs and ahead of only the Vancouver Canucks and the New York Islanders, who had only recently come into the league. It wasn't a very good time for me personally or for the Maple Leafs, especially after such an incredible high.

When we returned from Moscow, my agent, Alan Eagleson, thought it would be a good time to negotiate a new contract with owner Harold Ballard. I had scored thirty-eight goals in 1971–72, was coming off the Summit Series performance, and still had a lot of good years left in me as a player. Meanwhile, the WHA was still aggressively chasing NHL players. The league's Toronto franchise, the Toros, had obtained my WHA rights, and owner John F. Bassett called me one day and asked me what I was making, in hopes of luring me to the WHA fold. So I told him: I was making $75,000 a season, which was a decent salary, but there were players in the WHA who couldn't even make it in the NHL who were making more than that.

"I'll double it and give you a five-year, no-trade contract," he told me. "I'll throw in a signing bonus too." He even guaranteed I would be paid no matter what happened to the team or the league.

This was an offer that, at the time, was a very good one.

"Are you serious?" I asked.

"Yes, I'm serious," he replied.

I so desperately wanted my name on the Stanley Cup that I hadn't really been interested in going to the WHA. But when Bassett extended this offer, well, I had to look at it.

I sought advice from several people, and one person gave me plenty to think about. His name was Frank Mahovlich.

Mahovlich had been a Team Canada teammate, and, more importantly, he had played for the Maple Leafs – remember, he'd been involved in the trade that brought me to Toronto – so he knew the organization very well. When I asked him what he thought about me signing with the Toros, I also told him I was hesitant on account of my desire to one day win a Stanley Cup. He told me in no uncertain terms what he thought about that.

"You'll never win a Stanley Cup in Toronto as long as Harold Ballard is the owner," Mahovlich said. "The Leafs will never win with him, so you better get out of Toronto if you want to win a Stanley Cup one day, because it won't happen there."

He was adamant about that. And his words turned out to be prophetic. His advice strongly influenced my decision to sign with the Toros. I put Bassett in touch with Eagleson, and we came to an agreement that I would play with the Toros in 1974–75.

While this was going on, I was still playing with the Leafs, and as you can imagine, the news didn't go over very well with owner Harold Ballard – especially after Bassett let it slip at a party that they were both attending.

Like many people in hockey over the years, I'd had my share of run-ins with Ballard. Today's younger hockey fans may not remember him, but anyone who was around Maple Leaf Gardens in Ballard's heyday will tell you he could be impossible to deal with at times. He was one of a kind, to be sure.

Anyway, Ballard asked for a meeting with Eagleson and me, so we met him at the Hot Stove Lounge in Maple Leaf Gardens. With his typical arrogance, he tossed a contract at me for the same length and same money as the Toros were offering but with no signing bonus.

"Sign here!" he growled, probably thinking he was making a supreme sacrifice on my behalf. He had vowed he wasn't going to lose any more players to "the @#$@ WHA," and so he grudgingly offered the contract. But he was in for a surprise. I was tired of the way he had treated me and other players on our team, so I looked him right in the eye and gave it back to him.

"Harold, you take that contract and shove it!"

I'll never forget the look of rage in his face. He tossed over his chair and stormed out of the Hot Stove Lounge, and that signalled the end of my relationship – such as it was – with Harold Ballard, as well as my playing career as a Maple Leaf.

In retrospect, I shouldn't have done the deal while still under contract to the Leafs; it showed a lack of character and integrity on my part. And the Toros contract contained bonus clauses that were tied to my upcoming season with the Leafs. That wasn't right either, and in retrospect it should have never happened.

After my career ended, I tried to make up with Ballard several times, but he always refused to see me or communicate with me. I wrote him a letter apologizing for what I had said and done and asked him if we could make a fresh start. My spiritual mentor had told me I should not be offside with anyone, and I was farther offside with Ballard than with anyone, so I tried to reach out to him. He never replied.

Once, after I retired, I went into the Gardens to see a practice, but he wanted me out of the building. He even told Gord Stellick, the general manager at the time, to ask me to leave the building when I went to the Leafs dressing room to visit with coach John Brophy. Poor Gord felt really bad about that. He was apologetic and embarassed over the whole incident.

To top it all off, in 1981, Ballard sabotaged a job offer I'd received from Telemedia to do colour commentary on their radio broadcasts of Leafs games. After I retired, I had considered several different avenues, with broadcasting always at the back of mind, and this offer sounded like a good start. But Ballard would have no part of it, telling the radio people I wasn't allowed inside the building and that there was no way I was going to be a part of any broadcast from Maple Leaf Gardens involving the Toronto Maple Leafs.

I couldn't stand Harold Ballard back then, but I'm not proud of the way I acted during the contract hassles either. I certainly would have done things differently if I had the opportunity now – I didn't become a Christian until 1975 and didn't understand the concept of forgiveness. But that parting of the ways probably resulted, indirectly, in my going on to start my ministry later on because the broadcasting option was no longer open to me. Ballard blocking my progress turned out for the best. Though it really disappointed me at the time, I've learned a lot since then. Life is a journey – you learn as you go. I've learned far more in my life from failure and setbacks than I ever have from being successful – it's through adversity that you learn whether your faith is real. I now feel that God's hand played a part in everything that happened to me over the years. I also know that I have grown and matured over the years, and understand things from a different perspective today.

Knowing that – and knowing how it all worked out – well,

how could I still be bitter about what Harold Ballard did? Or what anyone else has done, either?

In fairness to Ballard, who acted in truly bizarre ways at times, he was never the same after his wife died in 1969. Without her stabilizing effect and wisdom, he lost his way and became a buffoon. It was really sad the way things turned out for him and I actually felt sorry for him.

I stayed healthier in 1973–74, appearing in sixty-nine games, and I had twenty-four goals and thirty-one assists for fifty-five points. The team bounced back too, finishing fourth in the East Division with eighty-six points under our new head coach, Red Kelly.

The last part of that season saw my ice time get reduced to much less than my usual time. It was quite frustrating as I had some good bonuses in my contract that I wouldn't be able to get as a result, and I always wondered why Kelly wasn't using me more.

I believe that Ballard was really forcing Kelly's hand when it came to decisions like this. One time, Kelly told me my problem was that my wrists weren't strong enough and that I should work on that instead of playing that night. My wrists weren't strong enough? That's how ridiculous the entire situation was at that point.

It was a truly frustrating time in a lot of ways. We made the playoffs that year but were eliminated by the Boston Bruins in four games, ending another season quite early. We were a decent team, but we lacked depth, so we were finished . . . and I was finished with the Leafs, and with the NHL, for that matter, until much later in my career.

It was time for a change, and that change came the next season.

RON ELLIS ON HENDERSON'S LEAVING FOR THE WHA

I have to say that I was very unhappy when Paul left for the World Hockey Association. We had already lost so many players to that league and now he was leaving, one of our best players. We were the best of friends back then; our wives were very close and so were our families. It was tough on me personally. It's at times like that where you find out how much the game is a business.

But I couldn't blame Paul for doing what he did, and it was perfectly understandable. He had his problems with Harold Ballard, and that was the big factor, but it was tough for him in Toronto right from the time he came back from Russia. When he was back in a Leafs uniform, expectations were sky high for him. But really, the Canada–Russia series was a once-in-a-lifetime scenario. Leaving for the WHA might have been the best thing for Paul, giving him a fresh start away from the intense media scrutiny he was getting in Toronto. I don't know if all the pressure on him and expectations for him were real – maybe Paul put a lot of that on himself. When he went [to the Toros,] it was a completely different environment for him and he could just relax and play the game again. There was no way he was going to do what he did in that series every night, and maybe some people in Toronto thought he was supposed to.

All I know is that I missed him personally and as a line-mate and a teammate.

CHAPTER TEN

SO MUCH HAS BEEN SAID ABOUT THE WORLD HOCKEY Association and the kind of league it was, and a lot of the stories about the league are pretty colourful. And there is no doubt about it, the WHA was a very colourful place.

I enjoyed playing in the WHA. It allowed me to get away from the stress of playing with the Leafs and, perhaps just as importantly, to get away from Harold Ballard.

Those last two seasons I spent with the Leafs after the Summit Series were tough on me, to the point that I developed an ulcer. I had more attention paid to me and was under as bright a spotlight as you can imagine during and after that series, so it was great to get away from that glare and get a chance to enjoy hockey again.

By 1974–75, the league was in its third season and had garnered a lot more credibility, having attracted such big-name NHL talent as Bobby Hull, J.C. Tremblay, Rejean Houle, Gerry Cheevers, Marc Tardif, Frank Mahovlich, and Gordie Howe. It was beginning to develop stars of its own too, like Ulf Nilsson, Anders Hedberg, and Gordie's sons, Mark and Marty Howe. The Toros played their home games at Maple Leaf Gardens, which obviously made me very comfortable. It really was an ideal situation for me at this time.

My first assignment in the new league was to play the Russians again, as the WHA had scheduled its own eight-game series for September 1974. I felt it was important to help the WHA showcase its talents, and I was really going to enjoy it this time around because I'd been through the experience before, and there wasn't nearly as much pressure on us this time. I even got to play tourist this time and visit some of the great historical museums in Moscow in between games.

The WHA was not on a par with the NHL by any stretch, but we showed it was a pretty solid league by the way we performed in that series. We battled the Russians very hard, and although the emotions and the stakes weren't as high as in 1972, it was a pretty good series and a watershed moment as far as the WHA's credibility was concerned.

I thought I played as well as I did in 1972, but this time I just couldn't seem to generate the goals like I did two years prior. Tretiak definitely had the upper hand this time around and was more familiar with my moves. I only managed to beat him twice. We opened the series with a 3–3 tie in Montreal, and followed with a 4–1 win in Toronto, but as it turned out, that would be the only victory we'd get in the series.

Our coach, Billy Harris, decided that everybody would play during the series, and I knew that cost us in game three in Winnipeg. He inserted eight new guys into the lineup for that game, and quite frankly that was a disaster. Everyone wound up playing in the series as promised, but it really took the edge off our game and we never did seem to hit our stride after that. Once again, we had likely invited too many players, and the guys who didn't play or were in and out of the lineup weren't very happy about it. It's so hard to get into a flow when you don't play all the time.

I played on a line with my old friend from the Detroit days, Bruce MacGregor, and Mike Walton, another good friend and former Leafs teammate. We had a lot of fun and scored a few goals, and MacGregor and I were killing penalties, something we had done for years.

We tied game four 5–5 in Vancouver, but the best we could do in the four games in Moscow was a 4–4 tie in game seven. We lost the other three games there, as the Soviets won the series 4–1–3.

The 1974–75 Toronto Toros were a pretty solid team. We finished in second place in the Canadian Division with eighty-eight points, trailing only the Quebec Nordiques. I played on a line with Wayne Dillon and "Shotgun" Tom Simpson, and I scored thirty goals and had thirty-three assists for sixty-three points in fifty-eight games. Frank Mahovlich was a star, of course, and the big Czech, Vaclav Nedomansky, was a forty-goal scorer with enormous talent. Our goalie was Gilles Gratton, one of the great all-time characters in hockey. Gilles believed that he was reincarnated, and his antics kept the mood nice and light all season long. The atmosphere was so laidback compared to the NHL, and there was really a great bunch of guys on that team and throughout the league.

In the playoffs, we were ousted by the San Diego Mariners in six games in the opening round, but my season ended well before then. A freak accident during a regular-season game forced me to the sidelines, as I collided with a Phoenix Roadrunner player who was headed to the bench during a game. We banged knees and I wound up tearing knee ligaments, which required season-ending surgery.

Billy Harris, the former Leaf who'd coached Team Canada '74, was the coach that year, and he was a terrific guy. He knew the game very well and we respected him, but we weren't nearly as strong as some of the better teams in the league, and he didn't finish the season as our coach.

I looked at the schedule at the start of the season and noticed that there were five times when we played home games on a Friday night, followed by Sunday night. The Leafs owned Saturday nights, of course, so we scheduled around them. At the time, we had a family home near Goderich, so I approached Harris with a proposal. If we won those Friday night games and I was the first star, I asked, would it be possible for me to skip the Saturday and Sunday morning skates so I could have more time off with my family over the weekend? Harris agreed. Well, talk about some good motivation for me: we won four of those five games and I was the first star in all four of the wins! So Eleanor and I would bundle up the kids into the car at, say, 11:00 p.m. on Friday and drive up to Goderich to enjoy some family time. We'd spend the weekend with our horse and cutter and snowmobiles, and I wouldn't have to be back until game time Sunday. It was such a treat to be able to have that kind of time to spend with your family on a weekend during hockey season! I remember saying to Eleanor several times, "Can you believe I get paid to do this?"

For the 1975–76 season, we had a new coach behind the bench: former Leaf Bobby Baun. We lost a few players to the NHL, including goalie Gilles Gratton, and we once again didn't have that strong a team as the season began, compared to some of the WHA's better clubs.

Baun was an honest and straightforward guy, but we just couldn't seem to get going that year and he wound up being fired before the season's end, which was a real shame. Gilles Leger replaced him, but that didn't help as we still wound up finishing in last place in the Canadian Division.

I had a decent year with twenty-six goals and twenty-nine assists for fifty-five points in sixty-five games, but we really didn't do much at all that season, which turned out to be the swan song for the WHA in Toronto. There was just no way we could compete with the Maple Leafs; even though we were playing in the same building, we might as well have been a million miles away from them in terms of popularity and attention. It's all Leafs, all the time, in Toronto today, and it was really the same back then.

After that season, Johnny Bassett decided the team would be moving to – of all places – Birmingham, Alabama! Wow, talk about a change of scenery. One of the terms of my contract with the Toros (soon to become the Bulls) was that I didn't have to relocate with the team if they moved farther than fifty miles from Toronto. In other words, the only place I *had* to move with the team would've been Hamilton. I didn't have any issues with moving, especially since Bassett had been so good to me, as a result of which I felt obligated to him from a moral perspective. Eleanor and I thought it would be a good learning experience for our family, as the children were thirteen, eleven, and six years old. As it would turn out, being in Birmingham was great for all of us. It was there that I would meet John Bradford, who became one of my mentors in helping me discover my deep spiritual roots. We wound up living there for eight years, and it ended up being a wonderful and rewarding experience.

So off we went to the Deep South, a different place for a hockey team, to be sure. But we had great fans at our games, and we found wonderful and solid friends who we still keep in contact with to this day.

I had twenty-three goals and twenty-five assists for forty-eight points that season in eighty-one games. The best part of it all was that all five of us really fell in love with the city. There was such a positive spirit in the "Bible Belt," and our lives revolved around the church and the many activities that it provided.

The city had a brand-new arena, and we would draw about 8,500 fans per game into it, which was pretty good for a southern city. The fans got into it as well. There was a real buzz about the team in the city, which made it kind of fun. Hardly anyone knew who Paul Henderson was, so I could go out in public and not be recognized – which suited me just fine. Eleanor was able to be herself instead of Paul Henderson's wife, and she really thrived there.

We built a home and settled into a very comfortable lifestyle in the city. We didn't have a great year on the ice as a team, but every player loved playing in Birmingham. The next season, 1977–78, we made the playoffs by finishing in sixth place in the East Division, and I had my best season in the WHA in terms of numbers, scoring thirty-seven goals and twenty-nine assists for sixty-six points. Glen Sonmor took over as coach, and we were a tough team that season, to be sure. I had never before been on a team that had so many fighters – we had four guys with more than two hundred minutes in penalties to prove it. None of those guys played more than half of the season either, so I was the peacemaker most of the time. I must have broken up dozens of fights that season, just trying to keep our guys from being thrown out of games!

One game in particular, at home against the Cincinnati Stingers, stands out. It became known as the "Thanksgiving Day Massacre." A massive brawl broke out just twelve seconds into the game, and it must have taken a good forty minutes or so to clean up the resulting mess. That was just the kind of team we had that year. We made a quick playoff exit, but that season was memorable in a lot of ways. The fans sure loved the fighting – and Peter Marrin and I sure played a lot because we killed the penalties, and there were a lot to kill.

In 1978–79, John Brophy became our head coach. He had gained considerable notoriety after a long career as a minor league defenceman in the Eastern Hockey League. He was the all-time leader in penalty minutes in the Eastern League by a wide margin, and he had thirty fights for every goal he scored! When he arrived, I didn't know what to expect because his reputation certainly preceded him. But remarkably, things seemed to settle down under Brophy, who treated me extremely well, and we really hit it off and became friends.

I was used in every situation that season – on the power play and penalty kill – while still taking my regular shift. I had a lot of respect for Brophy. He was a players' coach and the guys really loved him. If you worked hard for him, he would back you 100 percent, but he couldn't handle players who didn't give it their all. He was in incredible shape himself and had to work extremely hard as a player just to stay on teams, so he couldn't tolerate those who didn't share his work ethic or his passion for the game. Years later, he was coaching the Toronto Maple Leafs when Harold Ballard tossed me out of the Gardens, but Brophy called me aside and told me, "Paul, my door is always open for you." I never forgot that.

That season, Birmingham became known as the "Baby Bulls" because of how young some of the players were. Bassett had signed six eighteen-year-old players right out of junior hockey, including Rick Vaive, Rob Ramage, Craig Hartsburg, Michel Goulet, Gaston Gingras, and Pat Riggin. We also had Ken Linseman, Mark Napier, and Rod Langway. This strategy angered the NHL to no end, but it afforded these young kids a chance to get into pro hockey right away, and most of them did very well despite their tender ages and the fact they were playing in a pretty tough hockey league.

But despite all their potential, we just weren't good enough to compete with more experienced teams. We won thirty-two games and finished in last place. I had twenty-four goals and twenty-seven assists for fifty-one points, but we could see that the league was, in all probability, on its last legs. Talk of a merger between the NHL and WHA had been going on for quite a while, and while some teams seemed equipped to join the NHL, others certainly didn't. The Indianapolis Racers dropped out of the league after twenty-five games, leaving just six teams (we ended the season in sixth place). Playing for the Avco Cup sure didn't match competing for a Stanley

Cup, and due in part to a weakening American economy, the crowds had really shrunk in many of the WHA's markets.

That turned out to be the final season for the WHA, as the NHL agreed in March 1979 to swallow up four of the franchises – the Winnipeg Jets, New England Whalers, Quebec Nordiques, and Edmonton Oilers. Cincinnati and Birmingham didn't make the cut.

For the record, I thought the WHA was a pretty good league and that it was great for hockey players. It was a great place for young players to start their careers and for European players to get a chance to learn the North American game without the intense pressure of the National Hockey League. I was thirty-two years old when I jumped, and I was able to double my salary and enjoy many other benefits. I loved the guys and the coaches, and the games were so much fun they were almost like practices some nights.

The WHA certainly did a lot for players' salaries, which was a good thing for all players at the time. Up until then, players were at the mercy of the owners in the NHL, and the WHA provided a great alternative and some bargaining power – especially after Bobby Hull signed his million-dollar contract with the Winnipeg Jets and left Chicago. After I saw the way the Maple Leafs made Dave Keon fight over a small raise just to make $100,000 at the peak of his career, I realized the WHA would be a great thing for players' paycheques.

Some of hockey's all-time greats played in the WHA, from Gordie Howe, to Bobby Hull, to Dave Keon, and the league started the careers of players like Wayne Gretzky, Mark Messier, John Tonelli, Mark Howe, Mike Gartner, and Mike Liut, to mention just a few. It was a unique and fascinating time in hockey history. But the league was over with, and as the 1979–80 season approached, I had to decide what Paul Henderson would do.

I had thought about getting one more chance to play in the NHL before I retired, and I felt that I could still contribute at that level. But at the same time, I was extremely happy in Birmingham and, just as important for me at this stage of my life, so were Eleanor and the kids.

Cliff Fletcher, the general manager of the Atlanta Flames, called me during the off-season with an offer to join the Flames. It was tempting, but I wanted to stay in Birmingham, where the Flames' farm team would now be located. I signed, but with the proviso that I would stay in Birmingham and mentor the young kids in the lineup there. If the Flames ran into problems at any point in the season and needed me, I would go there – the two cities were about one hundred miles apart. It was a perfect solution for me and my family.

It was a decent year for me in Birmingham too, as I had seventeen goals and eighteen assists for thirty-five points in forty-seven games while helping Atlanta's future prospects develop. And sure enough, about halfway through the season, the Flames called me back up to the NHL.

It was a great thrill to be back in the NHL once again, a long-time removed from my years with the Red Wings and Maple Leafs. I got into thirty games that season and had seven goals and six assists for thirteen points. Two of those goals came in the same game, and that game turned out to be the last one I would ever play on Maple Leaf Gardens ice.

With my mother and family and friends in the crowd, I beat Toronto goaltender Mike Palmateer twice and was named the game's first star in a 5–2 win over the Leafs. As

I was announced as the game's first star and took a skate out onto the Gardens ice, I realized that it was a fantastic way for me to end my last game in Toronto.

RON ELLIS ON HENDERSON'S RETURN
TO MAPLE LEAF GARDENS

When Birmingham developed closer ties with the Atlanta Flames, Paul was called up to Atlanta and had a chance to play in the NHL once again. Well, they call him up just in time to play against us (the Maple Leafs) in Toronto. Paul tells the story here, but really I remember sitting on the bench that night just shaking my head. He was a good friend, I was so happy for him, but he comes back to Maple Leaf Gardens to play the Leafs, and what does he do? He scores a pair of goals and is named the game's first star! That game is so typical of Paul Henderson and what he is all about. He always did come up big in big situations. He beat my team that night, but I was really happy for my friend to play so well in a game like that.

Life was pretty good. I had the best of both worlds, getting another crack at the NHL after all those years and still keeping my home base in Birmingham, where Eleanor was working and thriving. As the 1980–81 season approached, however, there was news that the Flames were moving to Calgary. It would be another twenty years before big-league hockey returned to the Deep South.

As I've stated earlier, I loved Birmingham and the people there. It really turned out to be a great place for me and my family for a lot of reasons, and the friends we had there were terrific. I can't say enough about how much I enjoyed the environment there.

But I also have to be honest: I don't think hockey will ever go in the South. The sport is just not in people's blood there like it is here in Canada. It was popular for a while when I played there, but when the economy went south, so did hockey. I can only imagine how tough it would be to have a team there now. It sure was tough for the owners of the Thrashers, who sold the team to Winnipeg interests.

I mean no disrespect by saying that, but I am also very partial to hockey here in Canada. I would love to see a team in Quebec City again, and I was very supportive of Winnipeg before they got their team back. We have a passion for hockey in this country that cannot be matched. I even think there should be another team in southwestern Ontario. There is no doubt that a place like Hamilton or Kitchener could easily support an NHL team – or even a second team in Toronto, perhaps. When you see the interest and the passion for hockey in this part of the county, it doesn't make any sense to try to put teams in places that don't have that love of the game.

The Flames' impending move meant another decision for me. Fletcher offered me a two-year contract to to Calgary. He envisioned me as a role player, a veteran who could still see spot duty and come and work with the young kids on the team.

It was tempting. Calgary was, and still is, a great Canadian hockey city, and it would have been neat to be a part of the NHL coming there. But Eleanor and the kids clearly did not want to move again, so I declined and stayed in Birmingham for one more year, playing once again for John Brophy.

I knew the end of my career was nearing, and I decided it was time to put my family first. I didn't want to be a third- or fourth-line player, so I made what I consider to be the right decision for me at that time.

CHAPTER ELEVEN

THE BEST THING ABOUT SITTING DOWN AND LOOKING back over a life in hockey is the realization that I have been very fortunate in my career to have been able to play with and against some of the greatest players in NHL history. So I want to share some stories about these great players with you.

I am often asked to name the players I feel are the greatest players I ever played with, or against, in my career. I certainly don't have to think about that question very long. Right from the start, I was surrounded by hockey's legendary names. When I first came up to the Detroit Red Wings, we had seven Hall of Famers in our lineup. *Seven!* Terry Sawchuk in goal, Marcel Pronovost and Bill Gadsby on defence, and Norm Ullman, Alex Delvecchio, Gordie Howe, and Ted Lindsay up front. What a team we had there!

Imagine what a thrill it was for me the first time I walked into that dressing room and saw those guys. I made sure I got their autographs as I admired all of those great players so much, and to have had the chance to play with them all at the same time, well, that was something pretty special.

Bobby Orr was the greatest defenceman of my era, and probably the best to ever play the position. Goalies? Take your pick – Terry Sawchuk, Johnny Bower, Jacques Plante, Glenn Hall, and Gump Worsley – and I played with three of them – were all outstanding. Gordie Howe was known as Mr. Hockey and could do it all, and Jean Beliveau was one of my heroes – such a classy guy and a skilled player. The muscular Bobby Hull, racing down the wing and blasting slap shots at petrified goaltenders, was poetry in motion. But at the centre of my admiration and respect is the entire roster of Team Canada 1972 – a diverse group that Harry Sinden and John Ferguson melded into a team.

The generations of players that have come along since I retired are also outstanding – particularly Wayne Gretzky, Mario Lemieux, and Paul Coffey – but when you think about the players I faced like Orr, Sawchuk, Howe, Hull, Beliveau, et cetera, they were truly legendary players.

I guess I should say a few more words about Gordie Howe, the greatest player I ever played with. His nickname, Mr. Hockey, basically says it all. Howe was such a talented player and tremendous goal scorer, but it was the physical element of his game that separated him from the rest. Frankly, everybody was afraid of him, and with good reason – if you crossed him, he was liable to take your head off with one of those patented elbows of his!

Gordie loved playing the game, which explains why he played it for so long. He never gave up. I played against him in the WHA, and he played better at age fifty-one than he did when he was in his mid-thirties. He really was amazing.

When we were playing the Russians in Moscow in 1974, some guy took a run at Marty Howe, one of Gordie's sons. I watched it happen and thought immediately, This is not going to be good for you, buddy! Gordie took his number, and the next time they were on the ice together, Gordie gave him a two-hander across his forearm. The next day, the Russian player showed up at the arena with his arm in a cast. That was Gordie Howe – he took no prisoners, especially if you went after one of his sons.

He was feared because he could be so mean. Guys really tiptoed around him, just tried to stay out of his way, because if you got him riled up, it could be very dangerous for you. When he first came into the NHL, he went out of his way to beat the hell out of the two toughest guys on every team he faced. He made a point of it, just to tell everyone, "Don't mess with me," but it was the Red Wings who finally told him to knock it off because they needed him on the ice, not in the penalty box.

I was really leery of him after I got traded from Detroit to Toronto. He was notorious for giving it to former teammates – Pit Martin was a target after he was dealt to Boston and then Chicago – but he never gave me one of his infamous elbow shots, a fact for which I am eternally grateful, by the way!

Gordie did a lot for the game, but he didn't do anything for players' salaries. It was guys like him who kept salaries down because money was never a motivating factor for him – he just wanted to play. He never negotiated aggressively, although he could have asked for anything and, as the best player in the game, probably would have received it. Sid

Abel, the general manager and coach of the Wings for most of Gordie's prime years, was his former linemate and a longtime buddy. You'd think he might have told Gordie on the sly at some point that he could have earned much more money, but it was a business, and if Howe wasn't asking for a lot, well, the Red Wings sure weren't going to argue too much. I often wonder if some general managers got a bonus from their owners if they found a way to sign a player for as little as possible. It sure appeared to be the case at times, especially when it came to Howe.

Still, Gordie's place as one of the best players ever is secure – even though he didn't get paid nearly what he was worth throughout his legendary career.

Frank Mahovlich was another great player of a different sort. He was a very thoughtful guy, always introspective and keenly interested in learning. Not your typical NHL player. He always had an inquisitive mind and strong opinions about everything, which sometimes caused him to be a little misunderstood.

Even though he was an introvert, at times he could be very outgoing and friendly. You never knew which Frank you were going to get. He did march to a different drummer at times – in 1972, he didn't come with us to Sweden, for instance – but all in all he was a good teammate. He was so talented on the ice, and he had a really heavy shot.

Opposing goaltenders hated to face him because he could drill a shot and have it past them before they knew what had happened. And boy, when he wanted to turn it on, he could really go. But he struggled at times in Toronto under the intense spotlight and was often unhappy. As a result, he played some of his best hockey outside of Toronto, including a few impressive years in Montreal, during which he helped the Canadiens win a pair of Stanley Cups. He really enjoyed playing there, and playing with his brother Peter must have been very satisfying for them both.

I remember seeing him in Montreal once after he was traded, and he had the biggest smile on his face as he greeted me. "I feel like a kid again," he told me. Clearly, playing in Toronto for Punch Imlach wasn't for him, and getting out of there was the best thing that ever happened to him.

It did surprise me that he became a senator. But I can tell you that Frank Mahovlich treats that position with the utmost respect, and he does the very best job he can do. Frank is just too honourable a man not to give everything he has to every task he undertakes.

He was misunderstood often, but I have a lot of respect for him as a hockey player and a person. Still do, to this very day.

The name Tim Horton is known to many people today because of the coffee-and-doughnut chain. But the hockey player whose name is on those stores was a great one, and one of the strongest men I have ever met.

He was always doing curls and working on his powerful body. And the stories about him knocking down doors – all true, let me tell you. I've seen it happen!

Tim would have a few drinks and walk around the hotel, knocking on doors, looking to be invited into the other players' rooms. If he knocked on your door, you'd better let him in or else the door would come off its hinges. He would fire his huge chest against the door and break it down! And, of course, the unlucky occupants of the room would be the ones who had to pay for the damage, so whenever Tim knocked on our door, nobody ever told him to get lost. You did the smart thing and opened the door and let him in!

His death in a car accident in 1974 shocked the hockey world. I was with him the night he died. It was just after a game at Maple Leaf Gardens, when he was playing for the Buffalo Sabres. Eleanor, Tim, and I were walking back to our cars, which were parked in the players' parking lot a couple of blocks north of the Gardens on Church Street. With us was George McLagan, who worked for *Hockey Night in Canada* at the time.

We said our goodbyes, and hours later Tim was killed when he crashed his sports car on the way back to Buffalo. Eerily, less than a month later, George also died suddenly when he suffered carbon monoxide poisoning in his own car in his garage.

Both were cases of sad ends to great lives. Tim is still missed, and he won't be forgotten by those who knew him and his amazing strength.

There have been many tragic figures in the history of hockey, and former Leaf Brian "Spinner" Spencer is right at the top of the list.

Spencer was a good guy, but he was also a little different. He had a tough start to his life, and maybe he never got over that, but his brother became a commercial fisherman and a real solid citizen, so it wasn't all about upbringing, obviously.

Spinner was definitely off the wall, maybe even a little crazy. Other guys on the team tried to help him, as did I. But no matter what anyone did, he seemed destined to come to a sad ending. He was just a wild man – he couldn't get himself under control.

Once, after he had joined the New York Islanders, several of us met up with him in a club, and he had a .45-calibre gun in his jacket. That's the kind of weapon that could really cause some destruction. Nobody could possibly need to have something like that on them, but Spencer carried it with him, even in public. Once, Spinner's wife stayed over with Eleanor when we were on a road trip with the Leafs (the players' wives would often do that while we were away), and Eleanor discovered that *she* had a gun under her pillow while she slept! She didn't even seem to think it was a big deal when Eleanor found out; she just thought she needed it for safety and it was a good idea. Eleanor obviously didn't think it was a very good idea.

Brian and I played together for a couple of seasons on the Leafs. Spinner was then picked up by the New York Islanders, then traded to Buffalo and later to Pittsburgh. He didn't have a lot of talent, but he played with great heart and passion and was a good teammate.

His father made headlines when he tried to take over a TV station in British Columbia in order to get them to broadcast a Leafs game that Brian was playing in. He was killed by police officers in that incident.

When he could no longer play hockey, the lack of structure that comes with the hockey life caused his life to fall apart. He wound up living in a trailer in a Florida swamp and was charged with murder but acquitted.

He came and saw me in my office after that and asked me if I could help him find a job. His body was too banged up from his hockey career to do physical labour, but he was thinking of returning to Toronto or maybe Buffalo to try to restart his life. I told him to stay clean and keep away from drugs and I'd try to help, as I had a lot of connections in business and figured I could find him something. I know he also asked Rick Martin and Darryl Sittler for assistance at that time.

I told him I'd look around, and to stay in touch. But he just couldn't stay away from certain shady individuals, and about a month after I saw him, Brian "Spinner" Spencer was murdered.

When he died, the saddest thing was that it didn't surprise anybody. It really was a horrible shame, but it wasn't unexpected by any of us, which says a lot about how he was living his life.

It was hard to understand what was going through Spinner's head, but I do understand how even a professional athlete, someone who you think has everything going for them, can still be so unhappy. It's not just true of hockey players, it's true of anyone who has a lot of success in life. The popular assumption is that success will bring you happiness, or that being wealthy will bring you happiness. It just doesn't work that way. You have to learn how to handle life, both the good and the bad. And it's how you handle adversity and success that will define you. We'll all have success and failure at various points of our lives, and we need to learn how to handle both. Brian just couldn't handle life.

I know it's often difficult. The older I get, the more questions I seem to have about life – and the fewer answers. But over the years I've developed a lot more compassion for people who struggle, like Spinner. A lot of people who fall have nobody to pick them up, and unless you've walked in someone's shoes you really don't know what they're going through.

Looking pretty sharp, I must say – at the ripe old age of two.

The Lucknow Flax Flyers peewee team, circa 1954–55. I was a year or two younger than the rest of my teammates. Top row, left to right: Alan Chin, Bruce Baker, Gerry Mowbary, me (in the hat), Doug Schmidt. Bottom row, left to right: Fraser Ashton, Jim Peterson, Bill Robinson, Harold Howald, Barry McDonagh.

My yearbook photo from Lucknow District High School, 1957–58 school year.

SCHOOL DAYS 57-58

At the prom in Lucknow in 1961. Eleanor was the only girl in the room wearing an orchid, and look at me, decked out in my Hamilton Red Wings jacket.

From my rookie season as a member of the Detroit Red Wings, ready to go, in 1963–64.

From my second season with the Red Wings, circa 1964–65.

My 100th NHL goal, scored against the New York Rangers and
Gilles Villemure, at Maple Leaf Gardens. It was a nice one,
as I put a shot into the top corner.

My Team Canada picture, taken before the Series started in 1972.

With Eleanor in Moscow's famous Red Square,
taken during the 1972 Summit Series.

Hockey fans in Moscow liked autographs as much as Canadian fans did, and it was great to meet and mingle with some of them in Red Square.

МЕЖДУНАРОДНАЯ ТЕЛЕГРАММА

ГОСТИНИЦА ИНТУРИСТ КАНАДСКАЯ ХОККЕЙНАЯ КОМАНДА

МИНИСТЕРСТВО СВЯЗИ СССР

LT MR PAUL HENDERSON
TEAM CANADA SPORTS
PALACE MOSCOW (USSR)

ZCZC KSA146 FCB091 CN CD491
SUMS HL CANX 020 LUCKNOW ONT
CANADA 20 26 1528EDT

CONGRATULATIONS ON A FINE SERIES. WE ARE WATCHING
LUCKNOW AND AREA

A good luck telegram all the way from my hometown to Moscow.
It was so uplifting to know a whole country was behind us.

One of my favourite artists' renditions of *The Goal*, a beautiful job done by William Burdon.

The Henderson clan in the backyard of our house after the 1972 Summit Series, from a newspaper story that was done on us. Jill is in front, Jennifer on the left, and Heather on the right, with Eleanor at the back.

After The Goal was scored, the kids (and Wendy Sittler, who was watching them while we were gone) were besieged by autograph hunters. They finally had to put up a sign "We have NO autographs left!" Jill, the youngest, is in front, with Heather in the back in the middle, and Jennifer.

From my first season with the Toronto Toros of the WHA, 1974–75.

It was back to Russia for the 1974 WHA Series, and young Russian fans wanted to meet some of us. On the left is Mark Howe, then Tom Webster, and on my right, Ralph Backstrom.

I got called up to the Atlanta Flames in 1979–80 for one more taste of the NHL.

Proud of our family of "bikers" – from the left, our son-in-law Mike and daughter Jennifer Thompson, with their daughter-in-law Jesse and son Josh.

My daughter, Heather, and son-in-law, Alex, with their kids Zachary, Charlotte, and Brandon.

My daughter, Jill, with son-in-law Bryan, with their kids
Brynley, Logan, and Alton.

Proud of my Lucknow roots, as I pose with my badge from the 1958–59
Juvenile D finalist team by the arena there. The mural behind me is on a
storefront across from the rink.

The Henderson legacy will live on with grandsons Alton and Logan wearing "1972."

Eleanor and I posing with the famous No. 19 jersey inside the Henderson Jersey Homecoming Tour trailer.

I tried to help Brian, and now I try to help anyone who is in need the best I can. When I used to see beggars on the street, I'd never give them anything, always thinking, Why don't you get a job and get off the streets? But now I always do. I finally realized that many of these people begging could never find a job because of mental health issues. Eleanor and I now give significant money to charities and will continue to do so. We have been so blessed and fortunate, and we have never regretted helping others who are in need.

There are lots of reasons why people's lives unravel, but drugs, alcohol, and abuse are three of the main causes. They were a big part of Spinner's problems. All I know is that I've never met anybody who has said, "Gee, I'm really glad I was hooked on drugs" – or booze, for that matter.

We tried to help players in our day, and there is even more help available for them now. The National Hockey League Players' Association and the league are really trying to assist players with problems, and the people who run junior hockey are trying to do their part as well. It's a different ballgame now; they have some pretty good programs and it's much, much better than it was when Spencer played. Who knows whether he might have been able to be helped if he were playing in today's era? People have to admit that they have a problem first, and then ask for help – that's all there is to it. And a lot of them don't ask for help soon enough. That was true then and it's still true today. Whether it's Brian Spencer or one of the players who have struggled with demons in recent times, you have to want to be helped before anybody can help you.

———

Even in the midst of the most pressure-filled games and stress-ful times, you have to be able to laugh. When you were around a guy like Jim McKenny, you couldn't help but do so.

McKenny was – and still is – one of the funniest guys you are ever going to meet. He had the perfect sense of humour and knew the exact time to whip out that wit.

One time we were in the dressing room of the old Philadelphia Spectrum, and the mood was pretty tense. Back in those days, the Flyers were known as the Broad Street Bullies, and you knew that when you went in to play them there, you were going to get pounded. It's where the term "Philadelphia flu" comes from, as a lot of players came down with the malady just before they had to play the Flyers.

We were sitting in the dressing room before the game one night, and it was so quiet you could hear a pin drop. Our trainer, Guy Kinnear, walked in with some equipment and said, "It's as quiet as a morgue in here!"

Without missing a beat, McKenny came right back with a line that had us all howling on the floor.

"You'd be quiet too," McKenny said, "if you knew you were going to die in a half an hour."

It had us in stitches – probably because it captured perfectly the way most of us were feeling! It loosened us up to the point where we went out and played a great game, getting a rare 4–2 win over the Flyers in their own building. And nobody had to die to get the two points either.

A well-placed joke or a good line really takes the steam out of a pressure-filled situation. McKenny was one of the best guys for that.

———

I've seen and played with a lot of great players over the years, but when you think of competitive and intense players, Ted Lindsay would certainly come to mind very quickly.

His nickname was "Terrible Ted," and it was appropriate. He was just a little guy really, never weighed more than 175 pounds, but he sure was tough and never took a backward step when he was on the ice.

I remember one night in 1964 when Ted had come out of retirement after four years away from the game, when we were playing the Montreal Canadiens at home. Ted Harris of the Habs was a tall and rugged defenceman and a good fighter, but that didn't bother Lindsay. Ted challenged him that night and more than held his own, despite giving away at least three inches and thirty pounds, and he was pushing forty by then! But Lindsay only knew one way to play the game and that was at full blast, all out, even when he was at the tail end of his great career.

There were a lot of nights where a lot of guys just didn't want to play against Ted Lindsay, and who could blame them. It helped him to play with Gordie Howe for a lot of his career – a big guy who would come calling if there was any trouble. But Ted played with the persistence of a rattlesnake, took no prisoners, and never feared anybody out there.

Off the ice, Ted was just a terrific guy, a well-mannered man and gracious as can be. He was a wonderful teammate and one of the great wingers in the history of the game.

Similar to Ted Lindsay, John Ferguson was as nice a man off the ice as you could want to meet. He was actually kind of shy.

On the ice, though, look out! Something happened to John when he got out there. His eyes would glaze over and he'd turn into one of the toughest guys you'd ever play against. Without that transformation on the ice, he probably wouldn't have been the player that he was. And make no mistake about it; John Ferguson was a great player.

I remember one game against him when I was with Detroit. He came racing around his own net and I saw him coming with his head down. I hit him hard and knocked him flat on his back. It was a clean hit and I didn't get a penalty, so play continued.

Well, after the next whistle, just as they dropped the puck, he suckered me with a hard punch! We went at it – and I didn't win that fight either. That was the way he played – don't mess with him or he was going to come after you and everybody knew it. He was one of the best fighters in the NHL during his career, so you certainly didn't want him looking for you at any time.

He was as tough as they came and played with passion. Few people understood when he quit the game after just eight NHL seasons, but John was smart. He knew that a lot of fighters play a year too long, and that is always a bad thing for fighters. There are always younger guys coming along who are tough and strong and want to prove themselves, so he retired when he knew he should.

I only knew him as a fierce rival when he played, but then I got to know him very well when he was an assistant coach with Team Canada in 1972. John was a terrific guy, with a keen sense of humour, who really understood the game. He was a very valuable member of our team in 1972 and did a great job assisting Harry Sinden. I remember when we got to Moscow, he came and spoke to me personally.

"Paul, we need your line to play well over here," I remember him telling me. "With your speed, we know you are going to do well on the big ice surface."

I will never forget him for going out of his way to speak to me before those games. It did a lot for my confidence and really helped me be ready for what was coming.

He provided me with another great moment many years later when he made a point of telling me how much respect he had for the way I had lived my life after hockey. He was very complimentary, and it meant a lot coming from him.

John was a real gentleman and an important member of the 1972 team. He passed away on July 14, 2007. We miss him.

CHAPTER TWELVE

WHEN YOU START PLAYING IN THE NATIONAL HOCKEY League, you sometimes envision how your career is going to end. I certainly didn't see mine ending the way it did – playing on a team where the owners basically went bankrupt!

I stayed in Birmingham to play for one more season in 1980–81. It became obvious as we got down to the end of the season that the ownership was out of money. In February, they made the decision to cease operations.

All of us players came to the arena one morning to discover our equipment was gone – talk about a major wake-up call! That was it for the team, obviously, and it was the end of my playing career as well. I was thirty-eight years old and still in great shape, as I had always looked after myself, but it was time for me to move on and look for something else to do with my life.

I knew that my days as a top-flight player were over. I still had the skills and smarts to fill a role – I had even turned down an offer to play for the Flames earlier that season – but that wasn't for me at this stage. As I always did when faced with a significant crossroad in my life, I consulted with Eleanor and came to the right decision for us as a family. That decision was that it was time to walk away from the game of hockey that had been so good to us – for good.

Some players are devastated when they are cut from teams, especially if they want to continue playing hockey. I wound up quitting when I wanted to, not when somebody else told me it was time to quit, and looking back on it I played eighteen seasons of professional hockey into my late thirties. That's more than what I had hoped for starting out as a professional, so there was no reason to be uneasy about my decision to retire when I did.

Just because I was at peace with my decision to stop playing, however, didn't mean that I was at peace with being out of hockey. Any player will tell you that it's very hard to replace the buzz you get from being a professional hockey player. Half the fun of the game is in the dressing room, enjoying the camaraderie of your teammates, and you get to do that while playing a game that you love and making a decent living. Hockey is just a great lifestyle, both on and off the ice.

What exactly I would do next wasn't clear to me yet. I knew I had some time to make a decision that was right for all of us, but trying to decide what path to follow after I retired from playing hockey wasn't an easy task. I did know one thing – I certainly did not want to stay involved in hockey in any way, shape, or form. Cliff Fletcher, who was still running the Calgary Flames, asked me if I'd like an off-ice role, but that kind of thing – being a scout, coach, or manager – was never interesting to me. I loved to play the game, but the business side of the game had never appealed to me. The thought of trying to build a hockey team like he did, or scouting, or whatever, did nothing for me. I didn't have the passion for it, and if I don't have any passion for something, then there's no point in even attempting to do it, in my way of thinking. It just wasn't for me.

My problem with a lack of direction was a common one among players who had left the game. I felt I was mentally prepared to take on a new challenge, but a lot of ex-players weren't because they wasted a lot of their spare time when they were playing. Many of the players spent far too much time just playing cards. Those games were a good way for us to bond as teammates, but they sure didn't help us prepare in any way for a good career after we stopped playing. And of course there was the drinking and socializing after the games – far too many players turned to alcohol or drugs as a way to relieve the stress we were under, trying to perform on a nightly basis in front of huge crowds in the arena and even more watching on TV.

Alcohol use is quite well documented in hockey, in both the NHL and WHA. Its excessive use has played havoc with far too many players and ruined some lives, unfortunately. More than a few players I knew ran into problems on account of their lifestyles while still playing. Add to that the fact that there really isn't anything that can replace the rush of being a professional athlete after you retire. You go from having thousands of people cheering you on a nightly basis and making a tremendous living to – what? And when you are dealing with alcohol or drug issues, it makes it even tougher. I am so thankful that that is something I never had to deal with.

Things have changed a great deal now. First of all, the athletic conditioning and supervision of players have made it much tougher to be a huge partier and still play in today's NHL. Teams have also come a long way in helping players with their "exit strategies." Nobody really thought all that much about it when I retired as a player. You were pretty much on your own.

Today's player also has it so much better in terms of how much money they are making – millions and millions now, instead of thousands and thousands when I played – and agents certainly helped in that regard.

But now it was time for me to find something different to do with my life outside of the game.

A friend of mine was establishing an office for E.F. Hutton, the brokerage firm, and he offered me a position with him. After considering that possibility, I got the necessary training in New York so I could be a full-time broker by the spring.

The sales part of the job was right up my alley, and in my first three months working for them I opened up eighty-seven new accounts. It wasn't hockey, but it was a very competitive business, and I enjoyed it. But getting a green card in order to work legally in the United States turned out to be a real problem. I tried everything, but just couldn't make headway with U.S. immigration officials. Even with the help of a newspaper campaign pleading my cause in Alabama, I couldn't get the documentation I needed to work legally in the United States. NHL players could get seasonal work permits easily, but it was a different story for a Canadian wanting to work in the U.S. at that time.

This was a huge problem for me. One of my daughters was going to university in the United States at that time, and I had two other daughters in private schools, but I couldn't make a living in the United States. The logical option was to return to Canada. I was also considering a move into broadcasting, and there had been some interest in Canada. However, Harold Ballard had put a stop to that, so that door was closed for me. I was left with the dilemma of not being able to work in the United States and not being able to pursue a viable option for a career in Canada due to Ballard's interference.

My family didn't want to leave Birmingham, which was another issue. The kids were very content in school, and Eleanor just loved it. She was the entertainment chairman at our local church and was working at a local restaurant, as she'd developed into quite the gourmet cook. For years, Eleanor had raised our family and managed the household in the background of our marriage while I was Paul Henderson the hockey player, free to enjoy the limelight of an NHL career. Now she was gaining self-confidence and creating a wonderful life for herself. It was her turn to be able to do what she loved to do for once.

My family's happiness was very important to me – always was. Yet here I was, once again threatening to push their wants and needs to the background so I could explore a new venture. I just didn't want to do that. I made the decision to stay in the United States.

When we first got married, Eleanor and I both felt that this was a lifelong contract we were signing, till death do us part, and we both took it that way, so it should come as no surprise that we've been together for five decades.

I have nothing against divorced couples, by the way – sometimes people just marry the wrong person, and I can understand that. A couple of my sisters made the wrong choices, and that happens in life, but Eleanor and I took our vows seriously and have built a terrific life together.

We've been very, very fortunate over the years. Our marriage has always been solid and it still is today. We've been blessed with three great daughters, Heather (born in 1963), Jennifer (1965), and Jill (1970). We have seven grandchildren and are proud of our family, as they've all turned into such solid people.

Jennifer is so like her mother, Heather takes after me, and Jill, well, she's probably a combination of the two of us. They have brought such joy into our lives and given us all those wonderful grandchildren.

One advantage of a life in hockey is that you have summers off, so summers were for the family. I was also making good money as an NHL player, so we could afford to take vacations and travel a lot, and we did, taking the children with us. We were fortunate from that standpoint.

We weren't wealthy, but we enjoyed a very comfortable lifestyle. And we always stayed within our limits, were always smart with our money, and stayed out of debt – that dread of poverty never really left me, and it served us well over the years.

So as the years went by, our home became our oasis, and while I played and made us a living, Eleanor protected the home front. We were a great team.

I'm an impetuous person, very spontaneous and transparent. Eleanor was much more private, very thoughtful, and measured in her approach to life. We complemented each other, and she really helped me in so many areas of my life, especially helping me to become a more sensitive person, which I really needed to do. And nobody could put me in my place like Eleanor could. She certainly carried the velvet hammer in our household, and when she used it, I sure knew she was right to do it.

One time in particular – did she ever give it to me! I still remember that incident like it was yesterday. Like a lot of players in the off-season, I would drink a bit too much from time to time, although I usually kept it to a few beers. But one time I was playing in a baseball tournament in Goderich and wound up staying out very late. I came home after drinking far too much . . . and I was ripped, there's no other way to say it.

I slunk into the house, trying to be quiet, and she was waiting for me. There were three steps leading up into the house, and she was standing there and looking right at me – scaring me so badly I basically fell over myself and down the twelve basement steps to my right. Fortunately, I was so drunk and loose that I didn't get hurt or break anything!

She came after me and got about six inches from my face and proceeded to give me the tune-up of my life. She told me this kind of behaviour was not acceptable, I was a father and a husband now, and to come home late and drunk was no way for a responsible man to act. She really lit into me!

In no uncertain terms, she told me it was the last time I was ever going to disrespect her and our family by doing this, and ordered me upstairs to get into the shower and then into bed.

Well, have you ever seen what a whipped dog looks like? That was me. I meekly skulked off to the shower and then straight off to bed. When I needed a tune-up, Eleanor was always there to give it to me, and as always, she was right.

Eleanor was right that night, and I loved her so much I made sure I never had to be reminded of that again.

Like I said, marrying her was the best decision I ever made, as she was always there to steer me away from trouble and remind me what was right and what was wrong. And I always felt I could talk to her about anything, anything at all, and that's what made our marriage so strong. And after so many years of my career needs determining what my family would do, I knew it was time for me to put the needs and wants of Eleanor and the children at the top of the list.

There was only one thing for me to do now since I couldn't work legally, and that was to go to school. It would require cutting into our savings, as we would have no income coming in, but it was the best option at the time and turned out to be a great decision for us all. Still, hanging over the decision was the question of what I was going to do with the rest of my life, and what I should study. I had a bit of a sense of a calling, I suppose, but I had no anticipation, not one iota of thought, about getting into the ministry on a full-time basis, at least not yet.

I needed a challenge, something I could sink my teeth into, to take me out of my comfort zone. I was still wrestling with what to do, so I surrendered to God and decided that I would pursue the calling that was tugging at me and get some training in theology. I had become a follower of Jesus – a Christian – in 1975, and Eleanor and the children all followed suit shortly after. So I made the decision to enter the seminary and to ask God to give me direction from there. I was very nervous about it at first, especially about the financial implications – Christian work was certainly at the lower end of most pay schedules. But I saw the positive impact that faith had made on me and my family, and therefore I ulti-mately decided to spend my life making it count for the Lord.

That decision has led me to where I am today. I now believe that the Lord took me to Birmingham in order to mentor me and get me ready for my ministry. Today, many people think of Paul Henderson as the hockey player who became a very committed Christian..

In the late 1970s I was encouraged to come up with a pur-pose statement by my mentor, John Bradford; something that would summarize what the purpose of my life would be. I was challenged to think about the kind of man I wanted to become and just what exactly I wanted to do with my life.

It was a difficult process, but I like a challenge, and after eight or nine months of working on it, I had several pages of notes. But John told me that a good purpose statement was no more than one sentence. Being the competitive guy that I am, I decided I wanted to reduce mine down to the point where it was just several words. Therefore, I condensed several pages into four words.

My purpose statement is to be a "Godly world change agent."

Let me explain what *Godly* means. I want to live every day in a manner that is honouring and pleasing to the Lord. As far as *world* goes, I wanted to have a worldwide influ-ence (talk about dreaming big!). And as far as *change agent* goes, I wanted to help people make positive changes in their lives, exactly as my mentor, John Bradford, had done for me.

So, in four words, a "Godly world change agent" is what my purpose has been for more than thirty years now.

CHAPTER THIRTEEN

WHEN WE RETURNED TO CANADA IN 1984, MY FOCUS was simple: I wanted to create a safe place for men to ask any questions they had on spirituality.

Notice I said *spirituality*, not religion. There are so many misconceptions out there, so many biases, so many fears when it comes to men sharing their views and asking questions about how they can become more spiritual beings.

If you believe in eternity, then your life on this earth is nothing more than a blip, really. No matter how long a life you live, it's minuscule in the grand scheme of things. That's why you should learn to make the most of your time here on earth.

Although I didn't make the ultimate decision to work with a Christian ministry until after I retired from playing hockey, I suppose the roots were planted several years before that, after the high of the 1972 Canada–Russia series wore off, followed by the debilitating low that marked the next few years.

I returned to Canada as a hockey hero in late September 1972, but I have to admit that the years from 1973 to 1975 were difficult ones for me. My life had no direction and I was strangely discontented, even though most people would wonder why. I faced an internal struggle as to what I should do with my life and felt I was missing something, but on the surface, I really had everything anybody could want. I was a pro hockey player – which I loved being – and I was making good money. I was married to a terrific woman who loved me. I had three children, a beautiful home, and all the comforts a man could want. We had built the kind of life I had always envisioned.

The goal in Moscow lifted me to a level of celebrity in this country that I could have never imagined. I was living a dream after scoring that famous goal, and I knew that I would forever have a place in the annals of Canadian sport as a result.

And yet it wasn't enough somehow. Something was still lacking in my life. I enjoyed all the attention and the glory, but deep down I realized that I was looking for some real inner peace and contentment.

I made a common mistake. I thought that by attaining the goals I had set for myself early in life, I would be happy. I thought contentment should come from achievement. But at the height of my fame and accomplishment, a feeling of sadness came over me at times.

What does it take to make me happy? I wondered. What gives meaning to life? Why am I here? What am I really supposed to do? In short, I started asking myself the really important questions for the first time in my life.

I started asking some of these questions out loud, and it

seemed nobody could give me any answers. Many of the people I wound up asking had just as many questions as I did, and seemed just as discontented as I felt.

I was one of the most public people in the country at that time due to the 1972 series, but I wanted some privacy now. I was not content; I was frustrated, even angry at times and I was becoming more and more uncomfortable with myself. It wasn't a good feeling – I knew I had to change, but just how could I change and find some sense of deeper meaning to my life?

Religion had been a remote part of my life since childhood, as my mother went to the United Church in Lucknow. I believed in God, and would pray from time to time, but religion had no impact on my life. I'd go to church on occasion, but outside of that one hour on some Sundays, I lived my life as I pleased and was unaware that God wanted me to get to know Him and allow Him to be in my life as a guide and a comfort.

Finally, I met a man who had answers for me. That man was Mel Stevens.

Mel operated Teen Ranch, a Christian ranch just south of Orangeville, Ontario, and one season he gave all the Toronto Maple Leaf players beautiful leather-bound Bibles with the Leafs logo embossed on the cover of them. None of us took it very seriously. However, I began to pick up that Bible and read it after the 1972 series was over. I couldn't understand a lot of it, and certain parts of it really disturbed me instead of bringing me any kind of comfort. Instead of answers, I just had more questions.

In the winter of 1973, Mel came by my house and introduced himself, instead of doing it in a public place like Maple

Leaf Gardens. He asked me if I would participate as an instructor at a hockey school he ran at Teen Ranch.

"Sure, I'll do it," I said. "What does it pay?"

"It doesn't pay anything," he replied. "This is a Christian camp – we can't afford to pay anyone."

I thought to myself, Does this guy not know who I am? But we started talking and he seemed to me to be a very peaceful and confident person, so I listened to what he had to say. I guess the dissatisfaction I was feeling around that time was something others could sense as well because Mel told me I didn't seem to him like a very happy person. He had watched me interviewed on TV and noticed that I looked edgy, anxious, disgruntled, and irritated at times. After hearing that, I got to wondering if it was that noticeable to everybody. It really started me thinking once again about how I was living my life. I told him I was looking for something, as I felt something was missing in my life, but I didn't know what it was.

Mel told me I could get rid of the frustration and discontentment and also learn how to live "freely and lightly." He said he would help me look into the spiritual side of life and learn who God was. I was agreeable, so Mel started meeting with me weekly to talk about it. Mostly, I read the Bible and other books on Christianity and asked him questions – a lot of questions.

This went on for two years, and I spent hundreds of hours with Mel. Finally, in March 1975, I became a Christian by asking Jesus to be my Lord and saviour.

By the way, Eleanor did not like this one bit. I think she was fearful I was going to become fanatical about it all, and it would become an obsession and invade our marriage and our family. She didn't like Mel Stevens coming into our home, as she felt that going to church and trying to be good people was all the religion anyone needed in their lives.

Eleanor always went to church and I'd go occasionally, but before I really got serious about spirituality, we looked at going to church in very different ways. Her mom and dad always went to church, and she went with them, even playing the piano there. When we started our family we went to church together too. But she knew I wasn't really that interested, and it certainly had little effect on how I lived my life. Church was boring to me. There was no spiritual dimension to my life at all in those days, and I didn't see the point of it all. It did nothing for me. I went primarily because I was proud of being seen there with my family and I knew that Eleanor wanted me to go. We'd get dressed up for Easter and special events and I'd be pleased to see Eleanor and the kids looking great, but that was really the extent of it for me. Eleanor was the one who was really into going to church, while I was just along for the ride.

Things were about to change dramatically. Once I had made that decision to give my life to the Lord, Eleanor had to be told. She already didn't like Mel, and she was already suspicious of all the reading and studying I had been doing regarding spiritual issues, so she was wondering what was going on with me.

I was really nervous about telling her, but I finally sat her down one day and told her in simple terms that I had given my life to the Lord and was now a Christian.

Her reaction? She just looked at me and said, "Oh wonderful," and walked right out of the room. I didn't know what to say or do then, as I wasn't expecting that reaction at all.

Frankly, Eleanor was out of her comfort zone on this one. She was worried that I would sell all our worldly possessions and move to Africa or something ridiculous like that. There was tension between us, I must admit, as I started to embrace a new way of thinking while she wondered what in blazes was going on with her husband. She didn't understand the need that I was feeling to have to make changes in my life.

Mel had given Eleanor a Bible along the way, but she'd never bothered with it. So what did I do? I'd open it and leave it on her pillow at night so she couldn't help but see it! That is not a very good idea, by the way, when you are trying to get someone to talk about Christianity and what she believes in.

After a couple of months Eleanor started seeing a change in me, for the positive, and she started coming around as a result. She told me that I used to toss and turn in bed at night, and she would always fall asleep before me. Now that changed; I would fall asleep soon after my head hit the pillow as a calm and peacefulness seemed to come over me. She also noticed that I could sit and read for a couple of hours at a time, where before, it was only about fifteen minutes because I was so restless.

So she started to read the Bible seriously, and started to see what I had already seen. Every one of us needs a saviour if you want to go to heaven. She, too, began to study and embrace the Bible and what living a spiritual life really meant.

Eleanor had gone to church and was a religious person, but sitting in a church for an hour each week doesn't make you a Christian any more than sitting in a garage makes you a car. You become a Christian by really understanding the gospel, and soon she also invited Christ into her life as her Lord and saviour.

I am so thankful that our three girls also became Christians in 1975. Our daughter Heather went to Teen Ranch that summer and came home and announced to us that, at the age of twelve, she had given her life to the Lord as well. Our other daughters, Jennifer and Jill, also became Christians that fall. Today, all of us remain very committed followers of Jesus.

Christianity really made what was already a strong marriage and family life that much stronger. I believe if we had never become Christians we would still have a great marriage, as Eleanor and I have always loved and respected each other. But when a man becomes a Christian he becomes a better husband and father, as he understands the responsibility he has to the Lord regarding his family.

Until I took the time to study the Bible, I had an immature definition of love. The Bible (in 1 Corinthians 13:4–7) tells us the true definition of love: "Love is patient, love is kind. It does not envy, it does not boast, it is not proud. It does not dishonour others, it is not self-seeking, it is not easily angered, it keeps no record of wrongs. Love does not delight in evil but rejoices with the truth. It always protects, always trusts, always hopes, always perseveres. Love never fails."

I believe that becoming a Christian has helped me to become a better and more fulfilled person and gave me a spiritual awareness that was sorely lacking in my life. I consider it to be the most important decision I have made.

In later years, Eleanor and I went to marriage conferences and learned so much there. I learned, for instance, that I didn't know how to fight fair, and that I was more interested in winning the argument than I was in resolving the conflict in a respectful manner. I was not a good listener, and I learned that not communicating freely could seriously hamper your family relationships. For the last fifteen years, Eleanor and I have been speaking at marriage conferences and providing counselling to couples looking to find their way, and it has been very rewarding work. We get so much positive feedback. Becoming a Christian changed my life like nothing else ever did, and I am so grateful that my wife was able to share in that change with me.

And as a result, more than fifty years later, I am just as much in love with her as I was when I first met her in the grocery store. When young love turns into old love, it is the best love.

In 1973, I was still struggling to discover my faith fully. An example of the kind of question I plied Mel with: "Who is Jesus? Is He real or not?" For most of the next two years I studied all kinds of religious dogma and read an enormous amount of material on a wide variety of spiritual issues. I even spent some time with Jehovah's Witnesses. I became pretty knowledgeable in a lot of areas – or certainly knew a lot more than I did beforehand. As I studied and asked more and more questions, I started to embrace the concept of Christianity. I asked what a Christian is, and I learned that a Christian is someone who believes Jesus Christ is who He said He is. I came to understand that God really does love us, so much so that He decided to send His only son Jesus to die for us – He died for Paul Henderson.

This understanding came to me, but truthfully, it was a little frightening and intimidating at first for me. Accepting Christianity was like making a marriage commitment . . . I had to say "I do" to the Lord and make a decision, a commitment.

Well, it took me a long time to do that, and for the longest while I just couldn't bring myself to do it. And there were three reasons for that.

Reason one: ridicule. I had made fun of religious fanatics, those "born-again Christians," as I referred to them, not even knowing what that term meant, and here I was thinking of becoming a devout Christian myself. I was worried about losing my friends and about what people would think of me if I took this step.

Reason two: Christianity seemed to me to be all about dos and don'ts. How could I be a man's man – a professional hockey player – and be a Christian at the same time? There were so many dos that were required to be a Christian, and many of the don'ts were things that I liked to do!

Reason three: God expected me and every other Christian to be His ambassador. I discovered and read in the Bible that being a true Christian meant being a witness for Jesus. It would be embarrassing for me to have to do that, and I felt that I would never be comfortable doing that.

As I read and studied more about what being a Christian really meant, I was frankly disappointed in many ways with the kind of life I had lived up until this point. But I came around finally to understand that God loves me and wants me to get to know Him. God will forgive us for what we have done. God would forgive Paul Henderson for all the sins I had committed, and God's forgiveness comes without any exceptions.

It was March 12, 1975, while I was with the Toronto Toros of the World Hockey Association – but out of the lineup after having had knee surgery – that I had a conversation with God. I told Him that I had come to believe in Him, and I really wanted to have Him in my life. I asked for His forgiveness and asked Him to be my saviour and also my Lord, and to help me become the man He wanted me to be.

I then found myself saying, "Don't You expect me to tell anyone about this. This is just between You and me."

I wanted to be a "secret-service" Christian. I wanted a relationship with God without having to talk about it. But I knew deep down that that's not the way it works.

So, on that day, my new life began. I became a follower of Jesus, a Christian, and I thanked the Lord for loving me and forgiving me. I called Mel and told him. That day was his birthday, and he was happy for me.

Right up to this day, I am an avid student of the Bible. I have come to learn that Christianity isn't so much a religion as a relationship with God. There's a personal and intimate connection with the Lord when you walk with Him and make Him a part of your life on a daily basis.

Many other players over the years have come to know Jesus and have been willing to stand up and be a witness, including guys like my good friend Ron Ellis, Dave Burrows, Laurie Boschman, Mark Osborne, Stu Grimson, Mike Gartner, Doug Jarvis, Wes Jarvis, Mike Fisher, Dan Hamhuis, and many others. And their faith never interfered with or was an issue with their careers. And contrary to what many people may believe, being a Christian doesn't mean you can't be a tough performer on the ice or that you never take a penalty. Consider the statistics of these devout – yet solid and tough – Christian hockey players:

	GP	G	PTS	PIM
Ryan Walter	1,003	264	646	946
Mike Gartner	1,432	708	1,335	1,159
Laurie Boschman	1,009	229	577	2,260
Mark Osborne	919	212	531	1,152

Great coaches in both hockey and football are Christians as well, like Adam Rita (winner of a Grey Cup in 1991 with the Toronto Argonauts) and Wally Buono (winner of five Grey Cups with Calgary and British Columbia, most recently in 2011). Bob O'Billovich, a longtime successful CFL coach with the Toronto Argonauts and the Hamilton Tiger-Cats; Joe Gibbs, a Super Bowl winner with the Washington Redskins; and Dan Reeves, with Denver, also are well known for their beliefs. Lou Holtz, the longtime coach at Notre Dame University, and the great Tom Landry, of the Dallas Cowboys, are committed Christians.

On-field Christian leaders include CFL football players Damon Allen, Danny Barrett, and Kent Austin, and Toronto Argonauts Reggie Pleasant, Carl Brazley, and Pinball Clemons – who, of course, is renowned for his contributions to charities around the world. NFL stars Deion Sanders and the late Reggie White are also on this list, along with baseball stars such as Joe Carter, Greg Gagne, and Orel Hershiser, who were all successful players and Christians as well. Former NBA basketball star Dikembe Mutombo was public in his faith, and world-champion boxer George Foreman is also a Christian.

Then of course there is Tim Tebow, who became all the rage this past season. I am not the only athlete who has spoken openly about his faith. Many prominent players from various sports have done the same over the years. Perhaps no athlete has gotten as much publicity, however, as the former Denver Broncos quarterback and current New York Jets QB has in the past year or so.

Tebow's parents were missionaries, and he grew up in a missionary home. His parents were preaching the gospel everywhere they went, so with that kind of a background, his public persona is just a natural extension of who he is as a person.

I applaud a guy like that. He's such a competitor on the field, and he is as passionate about his faith as he is about his game. His style is not everybody's cup of tea. And it certainly generates a lot of discussion and publicity, both pro and con. How he is treated in the United States demonstrates that if a Christian speaks about his or her faith overtly, the press is going to take it on. That's just the way it is. The thing that irritates me about it all is that his ability to play is questioned as a result of his faith, which isn't fair.

I think Tim Tebow is an authentic guy and a very good athlete who tries to live the Christian life. And one benefit about a guy like him being so public about his faith is that it gets people thinking and talking about the issue.

I never gave any thought to the spiritual side of my life until I was challenged to do so at thirty years old, and there are a lot of people who have never thought about it. If someone like Tim Tebow comes forth and is willing to talk about his faith, perhaps that will get people to examine their own lives.

If you are inquisitive – if you ask, "What is this all about?" when it comes to your life – then at least you are thinking about what really matters in your life. If a Tim Tebow coming along causes a person with no spiritual background to at least look into it, then it's a positive result.

Sure, some people may dismiss it immediately after discussing it. You also get some crazies who are more embarrassing than anything else in the way they act about spiritual discussion. But it's all subjective; I'll let the Lord figure out whether all this publicity over an athlete discussing his religion so openly is a positive.

I do know this: some of my biggest critics when I first started talking about my faith are Christians themselves now, so how can that not be a positive?

I needed to see successful people who were also devoted Christians, especially when I first became a Christian. I needed to see that because, like many people, I thought Christianity was a crutch for those who couldn't succeed. Fortunately I met many successful Christian people in Birmingham, especially my mentor John Bradford and others. None of them, nor the great athletes I have just named, are just Christians on Sunday. They are Christians every day of the week. I was blown away by how successful and generous some of them were and still are. They say a sermon seen is worth a hundred preached, and these people lived their faith daily. I needed to see that, and I got that opportunity.

When I first became a Christian, I was still very immature regarding how to live the Christian life. A lot of players and other people didn't know how to handle me or what to think about me. Initially, I was way too aggressive, trying to convert people I met. In my zeal I wasn't being very intelligent about it. I was actually turning some people off, which was the opposite of what I was trying to accomplish. All I knew was that the Lord had changed me and I was convinced that other people's lives could be changed for the better as well.

One of my teammates on the Toronto Toros, Gavin Kirk, gave it to me straight one time. "Paul, you are a good guy, but you sure are a pain in the ass with all that talk about religion!" He was right. Looking back, I really came on far too strong back then.

John Bradford really helped me with that. There are times and places when you need to keep your mouth shut, I learned. You need to pick your spots and find the right time to talk about it. I learned that it was better to ask permission to talk about faith with someone – you shouldn't start giving answers to people who aren't asking any questions. I would give the Birmingham Bulls players a personalized Bible the way Mel Stevens had done for me and would talk about it when they were ready. That was a lesson well learned.

Becoming a Christian does not guarantee a trouble-free life. My faith underwent the ultimate test one night in December 1983 when Eleanor became very ill. That was – and still is – the worst night of my life. But surviving it really confirmed my faith.

Eleanor had not been feeling well at that time, and in fact had been experiencing stomach problems since June of that year. We were very concerned about her, as there had been a lot of cancer in Eleanor's family. We were especially fearful of her having ovarian cancer, so when she developed these stomach problems, our doctor – John Faucett – ordered some tests.

John was a great friend of ours in Birmingham at that time. We spent eight Christmas Eves together, and since we both had three daughters, we became fast friends. The tests came back and the results indicated that there was some abnormal cell growth and the decision was made that Eleanor would undergo a full hysterectomy.

As you can imagine, that's a tough situation, but as we

always did, we managed it through prayer and our faith in the Lord. We had a lot of people praying for her, including John Bradford and his wife, who were with us in her hospital room before the surgery. We laid hands on her and prayed for her, trusting that God would help her through this ordeal.

The surgery apparently went well, but later that evening Eleanor was having difficulty with her focus, she was in pain, and she was in and out of consciousness. The nurse finally had to call her doctor and tell him to come to the hospital immediately, as there was great concern.

I knew she was in real trouble when I saw her doctor perspiring as he attended to her, while she continued to slip in and out of consciousness. I will never forget holding her by the hand as she looked into my eyes and said to me, "I don't think I'm going to make it."

It was as if I'd been punched right in the stomach. This could not be happening – not to her, not at this time, and not like this. As three doctors now attended to her, I knew I had to leave the room and try to compose myself, as I was a nervous wreck by this point.

I walked down the hallway crying and feeling totally helpless. I had been a Christian since 1975, had given my life to the Lord, and now the most important person in the world to me was lying in a hospital bed, fighting for her life.

I was shaking my fist, staring up at the ceiling, and I remember yelling at God, "Don't You take her from me!" It was shortly after this that I sensed God was asking me to give Eleanor to Him. As I thought about that, I realized I had given everything important to me to the Lord over the past eight years – except I hadn't given Eleanor to Him yet.

It had taken me two full years to make the decision, but I had given my life to the Lord. As I've said, money was always a concern of mine, but we had started tithing and giving money generously. I had turned my finances over to Him, as important as they were to me. I knew that I had also given my three children to the Lord, but I just couldn't bring myself to give Eleanor to the Lord. I realized that night in the hospital that He was asking me for her.

I didn't hear a voice – not a tangible one – but a sense, a presence telling me that now God wanted me to give him Eleanor too. It was very clear to me then what He was asking for.

As I sat there crying and overcome with grief, suddenly a feeling of quietness came over me. I realized that I had a decision to make, and that the Lord was the one asking me to make that decision.

I slowly opened up my hand and said to the Lord, "I give Eleanor to You, God." I realized that she didn't really belong to me, she belonged to God. And I knew that there was nothing else in my life that I was keeping from Him now. At the same time, I prayed to him, "Please, please do not let her die." I told God that I didn't know how I could live without her, and I didn't know how I would be able to raise our three daughters without her. I begged God not to let her die, but I was also not nearly as fearful as I had been just a few minutes before. I understood that I had to trust in God no matter what – and that I had to give Him everything in my life, including the person who meant the most to me in the world. That was Eleanor.

I went back into that hospital room much more composed. I went to Eleanor's bedside and said, "Don't give up. You fight this!" I also told her how much I loved her and how much I and the children needed her. I stayed and prayed for her until the early morning hours, when she finally moved out of danger.

It was the worst night of my life by far. But it was also a pivotal experience for me, as I've never been the same in regards to my freedom and my relationship with God since then. There was still something in the way, something blocking the ultimate trust you need for a relationship with God . . . and I had to give Him Eleanor in the same way I had given Him my life, my finances, and my children.

I am not perfect, that's for sure. Since then, there have been times when I have taken her back, only to have to apologize to God and give her back to Him again. I now believe that God asks us for things when He knows we are mature enough to surrender them to Him, no matter what they may be.

The question is, "Do you trust God, or do you not trust God?" If you do, then you must surrender to Him completely, and that's what I did under the toughest circumstances for me imaginable.

For the past twenty-eight years I have worked for a Christian ministry now called Power to Change. I was given permission in 1985 to start a men's ministry under their umbrella that is now called LeaderImpact Group (LIG).

I felt a calling to reach out to men the same way Mel Stevens and John Bradford had done for me. I knew there were plenty of men just like me with little or no spiritual background looking for a place to discuss and get answers to help handle the stresses, pressures, and issues of life as they related to career, marriage, family relationships, and spirituality. I wanted to create a safe and friendly environment where men would have the freedom and confidence to talk about their own personal questions about life and how spirituality, from a biblical perspective, could answer many of their questions and needs.

I started with three men in downtown Toronto – two doctors and a businessman. We expanded to twelve men in a couple of months as they invited their friends or acquaintances to join our once-a-week sessions from 6:30 a.m. to 8:00 a.m. in a boardroom. I started another group in Hamilton doing the same thing. I simply replicated what John Bradford had modelled and taught me for three years in his group. The bottom line is we try to help men figure out who Jesus is and how He can influence their lives, which allows them to live life with purpose, direction, and fulfillment.

When I felt I had some men who could capably lead a group on their own, we would have a breakfast and ask the men in the group to consider asking some of their friends to come to a breakfast meeting and hear about what we were doing in our group. I would talk about my faith journey and the affect John Bradford had on me in his group. I would then ask three of the men already in the group to tell the audience why they came out to the group and how it was helping them. We would encourage the new attendees to consider joining a group. We asked them to come and "kick the tires" for four weeks and see if they were comfortable and if they found it beneficial.

Most of the men who came for the four weeks continued, and that is why we now have hundreds of men coming to groups in Toronto, Mississauga, Oakville, Burlington, Hamilton, Vaughan, Markham, Newmarket, Huntsville, Bracebridge, and Ottawa. As we have grown and others joined the staff, we have become a national organization with groups in other provinces as well.

We have developed some very gifted and talented mentor leaders over the years, and the ripple effect continues.

No one ever gets to the point where they know it all or don't need encouragement and support. The Bible says, "Iron sharpens iron, so one man sharpens the other." When you get twelve gifted men in a room, there is great discernment and insight, and everyone benefits from the collective wisdom. Many men will give their small group the credit for their development and spiritual maturity.

Eleanor and I have spoken at weekend marriage conferences for the last fifteen years teaching couples about biblical principles that allow couples to have a game plan to achieve oneness and harmony within a solid marriage. I believe having a great marriage is one of the most difficult and challenging tasks that we take on; everyone needs help and instruction to get through the tough times. All marriages go through difficult and challenging times, but many couples have no clue how to deal with them and keep the marriage together. We are able to give them hope and solid principles to work through their issues and develop love and deep intimacy with each other.

I have had the opportunity to speak about my faith and ministry hundreds of times in every province in Canada and in more than twenty other countries.

Many of the men in our groups have also joined us on international projects and have spoken on how they operate their business with biblical principles and what part their faith plays in allowing them to handle the challenges of their business world.

I also love the many and varied motivational speaking opportunities I get to address corporations about leadership, teamwork, mentoring, making it happen, and winning.

Needless to say, I have spoken at more fundraiser and charity events than I probably should have, at least from my wife's perspective.

CHAPTER FOURTEEN

When you decide to give your life to the Lord, that is what you do. I have tried to serve Him in every way since I made that decision, and that has been the goal of my life's work since then.

I have had the opportunity to help other people with their own spiritual searches since then, in the same way that my mentor, John Bradford, did for me many years ago.

Some of the men I have worked with over the years were kind enough to provide their thoughts on their own journeys with me, and I am honoured to share some of their observations with you in this chapter.

BRIAN McCARTHY – Insurance Executive

When I first saw Paul Henderson at an outreach breakfast, it was a great thing. One of the best memories of my life was Paul scoring that goal with the seconds ticking down. I left the hall where I was watching the game thinking, I am so proud to be Canadian! Now I was meeting him. He spoke of Christian faith and coming to the Lord in a meaningful way, but with me being Catholic, naturally I thought he was talking to everyone else because I never missed mass. He invited us to join a men's group. I didn't join. However, after five breakfasts and hearing Paul five times I decided to give it a try. I met ten strangers from different walks of life and soon became great friends! We shared all the struggles men face together! I realized there is so much more to life with Christ at the centre!

My relationship with Paul strengthened when my career and my personal life met with disaster. My daughter had a CAT scan and a growth on her brain was discovered. The public company I ran closed its door and I was blamed. I was facing four years of legal battles with no job and a daughter in danger. Paul and Fred Christmas, as well as the men in my group, rallied around me and because of my renewed stronger faith I was able to be the husband and father that my family needed during this period. My daughter's growth is benign, I got a new job, and my legal problems are behind me. The hardest years of my life so far are now behind me. Besides the phone calls from Paul from time to time, the promise that he would pray for me every day made such an impact on me that I never doubted I would get through.

Today, I run a men's group. I oversee the Oakville area for the ministry and I consider the ministry "my" ministry. I have to get the word out to as many men as possible. Get Christ in their lives, meet with other men to sustain them in the hard times, and help others in the good times. Most of all, they explore their faith. We all have a mind, body, and *soul; what are we doing for our souls? Paul today isn't well and this too has affected me. I see a real man who is facing this struggle with character and grace but mostly great faith. I watch closely and I want to finish well. I am so blessed to have a guy who shows me it can be done and how to do it to be a beacon for others.*

It isn't hard to figure out where I would be if I didn't have Paul in my life. I wouldn't have had the faith and courage to meet my challenges. I know it was my faith in Christ and the resources He provided that got me through. There is alcohol abuse in my family but never me; there was despair and defeat in my family but I never even considered it. When people ask how I could handle all the pressure and still get four kids through university, I always feel like a bit of a fraud because it wasn't that hard when the creator of the universe is with me.

I am shy to this day of Paul Henderson, but I don't know where I'd be without him.

SOL STERN – Doctor

Paul had a dramatic effect on my life. I learned that God was calling me to become a completed Jew through the acceptance of Jesus as the Messiah.

Paul's love of the Bible led me to study it as well and appreciate God's word. After I became a believer, I began to give presentations to other physicians about pain management and have hopefully had a positive effect on the pain control of many patients in Canada.

I continue to be actively involved in our church, and my wife has even become an elder. I gave more than one hundred presentations last year on pain management and continue to have a full family practice in my community.

Paul influenced me in so many ways, but the thing that has impressed me the most is his love and adoration of both Jesus and his family.

STEPHEN OSTAPCHUK – State Farm Insurance Owner/Operator

I've known Paul for twenty-seven years. We met at church just after my wife and I had married and when Paul had just got back from Birmingham.

My wife, Cathie, and Eleanor and Paul and I developed a strong friendship over the next few years. When our son was born, Paul was one of the first to celebrate with us and hold Jordan in his arms. He has continued to be a mentor to Jordan throughout his journey over the last twenty-five years.

Whether it was sharing a meal, a game of squash, or serious conversations about our faith, Paul modelled extraordinary commitment to his faith, his values, his marriage and family, and our friendship. He was competing for a higher goal than the Goal of the Century, which gave him fame and glory. He was and is to this day a true mentor.

He encouraged me to get involved with one of his first discipleship groups in downtown Toronto twenty-seven years ago. Paul would pick me up to drive downtown and he would always check in with me in the car, asking if I had my memory work and my homework done! (He has mellowed since.) Many of the memory verses I learned in that time I still hold close to my heart and recite often in challenging times. Paul taught me about conversational prayer and daily quiet times, which I have continued to have every morning.

Paul's influence has challenged me to be the husband, father, employer, and friend that God wants me to be. Now, Thursday morning is my best day of the week as I facilitate a men's group of my own (for seventeen years), and I am encouraged to see other men grow in their faith as Paul has challenged me to do through his impact on my life. He will always be a competitive athlete on and off the ice, as I can attest to when we golf together, but he presses on for the goal of a higher calling – one where he will enter heaven, with a life poured out for others, and receive his heaven's hall of fame commendation of "well done, good and faithful servant." Paul has always been there with discernment and wise counsel in times of need for me and my family, and he will always have a special spot in our hearts.

DON WEISS – Retired Pension Fund Manager

When Paul Henderson invited me to join a men's group, I have to admit that I was not too enthusiastic about the idea of getting up early in the morning to sit down with a bunch of men to discuss spiritual values. That just did not appeal to me. I had tried an early men's Bible study before and found it an absolute chore to start off the day this way. The result was . . . I didn't last long.

Paul wears his spiritual life on his sleeve, which I admire. It wasn't my style at the time, but I discovered it is infectious. I've moved a long way to wearing my spiritual life on my sleeve. For me, the discovery group meetings turned into "I can't wait to come back next week." And I know the feeling is mutual for many men in our group.

Now it has been years since I first tried on a discovery group, and my love and appreciation of groups continues to grow. I'm thankful to Paul for inviting me and know I have a closer relationship with Christ today and a greater hunger to learn more about Him. My purpose in life has become more clear to me than ever. Over time, I've increased my involvement in discovery groups and learned what a difference it can make to your life. I say "treat yourself" to a discovery group . . . it's one of the best presents you can give yourself.

LES McFARLANE – Business Owner, Entrepreneur

I have learned to be more disciplined in life. Paul, you are an outstanding role model. You show discipline in your spiritual walk, your physical workouts, and your driving desire to improve your mental capacity – such as memorization, reading, crosswords, et cetera.

I am more serious about my faith. I want to finish this life well. I try to memorize more scripture and read good spiritual books. I try to set time aside at the end of the day to evaluate my day. Did I live this day as Jesus would have me?

I love your enthusiasm about your relationship with Jesus. You are so positive and not afraid to say the right word at the right time. You have a zest for life and your attitude toward your cancer is refreshing, uplifting, and without fear.

You are an encourager – like Barnabas. Your messages are

so positive and encouraging. It means a great deal to me to know that you faithfully pray for me. If we ever go to war, I want you on my side!

Blessings, Paul!

DENIS FRAPPIER – AMJ Campbell Owner/Operator

Having lost my earthly father who I revered for several years at the age of eighteen, I have now gained my Heavenly Father Jesus Christ who I call Lord!

My daily spiritual walk with Lord Jesus Christ has instilled a great sense of calmness and gentleness into my everyday life, as this spiritual covenant has removed the letter "D" in front of the word "Anger"!

I am in touch (pray) with my Heavenly Father every day, and that provides me with great discipline, focus, and leadership. In turn, He provides me wirth peace, security, and love.

I lead a LeaderImpact Group (LIG) at AMJ Markham and I'm also the York Region City Team Leader. I am also a member of the Partner Development Committee.

LIG has been the catalyst for transforming my life. Despite trying, I could not do it by myself as I could not deal with it on my own! My Christian faith is the core, and my participation in a weekly discovery group helps me protect the core day in and day out!

STUART CAMPBELL – Business Consultant

I was transformed and became a new person. I learned that God, who laid the foundation of the earth and whose hands made the heavens, also created me in His image. By inviting

His son, Jesus Christ, into my heart, I have the right to be God's child and am able to enjoy a personal relationship with God as my Father.

I set aside a quiet time every morning to spend uninterrupted time with God, reading his word, and through prayer, hand my day over to Him so that I may serve Him. I memorize scripture; I pray; I am always aware of God's guidance. The difference is that it is not about me; rather, it's about glorifying and praising God.

I am a member of a vibrant men's group that meets weekly and am a deacon at my church. I witness freely to people interested in learning about or exploring spiritual questions.

Paul Henderson's ministry ignited the Holy Spirit in my life. I became a new person – a spiritual leader at home; a caring, loving husband; a servant leader at work; a caring friend. I am forever grateful for how God touched me and called out to me through Paul's ministry.

BRUCE ETHERINGTON – Insurance and Wealth Manager

You changed my life by introducing me to the truth of biblical scripture and the reality of Jesus Christ. I began to move away from worshipping self and all things of this world to Jesus and the values of His Kingdom – loving others as He loves me.

I live a different lifestyle from that of twenty-five years ago – Christ-centred rather than self-centred, and while in no way am I perfect, I am also not the person I used to be and am moving closer, I believe, to becoming the person God wants me to be in Christ Jesus. That is a person who puts others before self, prays and reads God's word daily, and *recognizes that God has given me many blessings with which to do His will – which I try and focus upon daily while rejoicing in the fact that my Saviour lives and has forgiven me all my sins and granted me eternal life!*

Some examples are: I try to love others as God loves me, which involves the forgiveness of those who have hurt or offended me; I practise daily discipline of quiet time, prayer, and reading God's word; and I am involved with and a supporter of many Christian charities and organizations.

I recently launched a National Mentoring Program for insurance-based financial advisers, which teaches them how to "fish in deep waters" in accordance with biblical principles. I always proclaim Jesus from the public platform whenever and wherever I speak. To Him be the glory!

I am very grateful that you had the courage to ask me how my spiritual life was twenty-five years ago, as it not only changed my life, as mentioned, but it resulted in my salvation. THANK YOU MY DEAR FRIEND!

BRUCE BOWSER – CEO, AMJ Campbell Ltd.

Paul, having spent half of my thirties and all of my forties in one of your groups, I can attest to the significant impact it has made in my role as a business leader and as a father. I quickly learned from other men in the group that life does not require you to make the same mistakes that someone else made just so that you can say you learned by the school of hard knocks. The truth is that many of the men in my groups, especially those older and more mature than myself, were able to help me avoid pitfalls and mistakes that they had made.

As men, we tend to think that we have not learned something well unless we got bruised or scraped in the process, when in fact simple truths that are shared by men who have been there can actually provide you with the same learning opportunity minus the damage. I also learned from Paul, having heard one of his favourite passages thousands of times, that iron sharpens iron, and that the sad reality is that there are very few venues in a man's life where he can experience the type of exchange, learning, and support that comes from being in a group like so many of us were.

There have been many times in my life where I have met someone who I knew needed the type of learning, support, encouragement, and direction that comes from a group, and being part of Paul's network allowed me to invite them to join. In my own business, I know that this has resulted in some of our most senior people coming to faith and experiencing life-changing results through their participation in a group that we were able to place them in. Long-term, I believe that most men who have had the opportunity to belong to a group will look back in the later years of their lives and realize the impact that their participation had on their own family lives, the lives of those whom they interacted with in the group, and the generations of children whose lives will be forever different as a result of a decision their father, grandfather, or great-grandfather made to belong to a group.

Being a part of a group helped me to develop a disciplined prayer life, a much deeper and more applicable understanding of the Bible, and a profound understanding and appreciation for the many common threads that intertwine us as men living in the business world. Being part of a group is like being tethered to a safe place where accountability, support, *learning, and encouragement all become something you look forward to and yearn for when you are away.*

I would also add that the life and work of the group is not confined to one morning a week, but in fact it has created bonds of friendship among men and families that will last a lifetime and touch people in ways that we could never track or imagine.

STUART MacMILLAN – Company President

The impact to me was centred around discipline. While I was successful in the business world, I was not quite as adept at applying the disciplined principles I used in business to my personal life. Through Paul and the group, we had enough open, frank conversation in which I was able to be honest to my colleagues – and, more importantly, myself – about the gaps in consistency in my behaviour. I was also able to understand that stress is created by a multiplicity of purpose. If I am able to align everything in my life to a central purpose – in my case, being a Christ follower – much of the stress disappears.

I am disciplined about daily devotions with my wife, Debra. I try to align all my decision making with my central purpose of being a Christ follower. I ensure that disciplined principles from my work life (being present, being an encourager, maximizing my time) are also principles that I follow in my personal life.

Paul has touched me in a way I would allow very few other people to. In that he has the combination of tough-minded accountability as well as compassion, I was able to address weaknesses in my life without feeling like I was being judged. He has become a model of the kind of man I want to be, and – as I turn fifty this year and am halfway through the earthly portion of my existence – has given me the drive to finish strong *and do the next half way better!*

DR. ROBERT INMAN – Doctor

Paul, it is hard to articulate how important the group was for me at that point in my walk, but here is one comment that comes to mind at once.

You can hear all the advice about personal prayer time, and read all the books on the importance of a personal devotional time becoming a habit, but until you personally witness the transformative power of this spiritual discipline, it will not imprint itself into a daily routine. Experiencing with other men in a discovery group what this transformative habit looks like, how to do it, how to stick with it, changes the course and the depth of our spiritual journey. And encouragement has always been recognized as the by-product of meeting together (Hebrews 10:25).

MR. JUSTICE JAMES TURNBULL

Paul, you have to be kidding. I could write a book!

As you know, the group significantly changed my life. For the first time in my life, I was challenged to read the Bible, discuss it, memorize scripture, and actually consider its impact on my life. It became clear to me that putting Jesus Christ in the centre of my life was essential to a meaningful and significant life. I was taught how to share my faith in a non-offensive but clear manner. I learned the importance of having a good church and having a close circle of Christian men in whom I could confide and whose counsel I could seek.

And most importantly, I learned what living an abundant life is really all about. I try to start each day with a "quiet time" as Paul encouraged us to do. I must confess that with the rush of life and the many demands on me, I am not as faithful in doing that as I should be.

After leaving the group led by Paul, he urged me to start my own group. I did that and have led or been actively involved in a group ever since . . . which is about twenty-five years now.

Because of being in Paul's group, I was asked to share my faith at a Billy Graham Crusade in October 1988. On that evening, I met a lady who arranged for the men in the group I was leading at that time to take a mission trip to Haiti in August 1989. Since then, I have been back to Haiti more than forty times and worked with other volunteers to build twenty-five Christian schools in the north of Haiti where approximately seven thousand children now receive a Christian education. We have also built two churches and an orphanage where thirty-four children are fed, housed, and cared for largely due to donations from generous Canadians. We have seen the lives of many Canadians changed significantly when they have seen and smelled and felt the plight of the poor Haitian people.

Many of them have made decisions to accept Jesus Christ in their lives as a result of their exposure to that country.

Today, my faith is more important to me than ever as I deal with the multitude of concerns that confront me as a father, husband, and friend. In my role as a Superior Court judge, I daily ask God to give me wisdom before I enter the courtroom because virtually every decision I render significantly affects the lives of others.

RICHARD BENNETT – Lawyer

I met Paul in 1994. The thing that resonated the most with me about his testimony is that he came into a relationship with Jesus Christ at a time when he had everything the secular world had to offer, and yet had this thirst to fill a void. I have always believed that people will not listen to what you say unless it matches what you do. Over the years, Paul has consistently demonstrated that his actions replicate what he tries to impart to others. Nothing has more poignantly shown this than the genuine peace and joy he shows while battling cancer.

Paul invited me to be a member of his morning group eleven years ago, telling us at the start that his objective was to mentor each of us to become leaders. After three years, I felt that I was ready to lead my own and have done so on a weekly basis since then.

As a direct result of Paul's impact on me, I have tried to "pay it forward," and now men whom I have mentored understand and practise openness, are willing to share and address deep issues with other men, to have other men hold them accountable, and are better husbands and fathers and therefore better men. This, in turn, stirs the desire within them to share their growth with other men.

Paul, like any of us, is not perfect but, through example, demonstrates that if we strive for perfection, we can achieve excellence. He has taught me the value of prayer, and over the last eleven years there are few days when we have not prayed for one another. He lives his mantra that "there can be no impact without contact" through regular communication and making you feel that he has all the time in the world for you despite having contact with dozens on a daily basis.

When I mentioned to my wife that Paul was looking for feedback as to how he had influenced me, she volunteered the following observations of how I have grown as a husband as a result of his impact:

When with a group of couples, she feels that no woman in the room is loved more than she, a major change that is a result of Paul sharing that about how he makes Eleanor feel.

Paul is a natural leader and she feels that through his mentorship, my once latent leadership qualities have blossomed at home, professionally, and in mentoring men and other couples.

One of Paul's favourite Bible verses is "iron sharpens iron," and Deborah and I are certain that, as a result of his influence, I am a far better husband, father, and man than I would have been had I not had the opportunity of developing the relationship with a man who, as a result of scoring "the Goal of the Century," has selflessly used that springboard to positively affect countless lives over the past forty years and who I am humbled to call one of my best friends.

DAVE TOYCEN – President, World Vision Canada

1) Paul has been a tremendous example of someone who has leveraged his status as one of Canada's most iconic sports figures to accomplish things that have made a significant impact on others. He has taught me that every one of us has a responsibility to take what we have been given by God and use it to influence others to make this world a better place. If it's humanly possible, Paul has enhanced God's reputation across Canada. He has been courageous in sharing his faith in Jesus Christ with anyone who would listen. It challenged me to speak more boldly about my faith as well.

2) Paul has taught me grace when life gets tough. His confidence in God to see him through is both awesome and inspiring. It's been a reminder to me that our faith is most vibrant when we are tested by life's challenges and mysteries.

3) Paul's eagerness to learn especially in matters of Christian faith has brought a balance and maturity to the natural enthusiasm that God has given him. My years in one of his leadership groups increased my confidence and encouraged my spiritual disciplines. He has reaffirmed my belief that growing as Christians is just as important as becoming a Christian.

4) Paul's love and respect for his wife, Eleanor, has always set an example that I want to emulate. His willingness to share his shortcomings, speak frankly about his journey, and then challenge men to take their marriages and families seriously has set a new standard.

5) In my leadership role, Paul has always been an encourager. His passion and goal orientation have pushed me to be better. Paul's example has helped me stay firm in my commitment as a Christian leader. I believe my leadership at World Vision Canada has benefited because of his support.

6) Most importantly, Paul has been a friend to me. His transparency, willingness to listen, and life experience are a gift.

I hope this encourages you and expresses my admiration for who you are and what you do.

GARY CASCONE – President, Zicon Construction

Some of the impact of my relationship with Paul and the ministry are as follows:

1) Paul was the one who courageously spoke to me about the gospel, and when I asked questions he followed up by inviting my wife and me to his home to discuss biblical and spiritual matters in depth.

2) From the first moment that he witnessed to me until the time I accepted Christ was a week and a half.

3) Upon Paul's return to Canada, he became part of the ministry and almost immediately began a discipleship group modelled after the one he had attended in Birmingham, Alabama.

4) He invited me to be part of that first group using the master life series material. This material was similar to the purpose for living material that we use today.

4) He caught a vision to disciple men and challenge them to become vehicles and ambassadors for Christ. The challenge was also to be available to go wherever God called us to, anywhere in the world.

5) As Paul matured in his life as a Christian, his challenge also matured to the point of helping me realize that I must listen to the challenges put to me by the holy spirit of God.

6) I also know that I can always count on him to be consistent and honest with praise and criticism.

7) I know that he prays for me on a regular basis, and I am encouraged by that.

8) He has always encouraged me to stay in God's word and step out in faith based on the leading of the Holy Spirit.

9) Through the ministry, I have been introduced to many Godly men, such as Bill Bright and Tony Campolo.

Some of the things that I do differently today are as follows:

1) After thirty-two years as a Christian and a friend of Paul's, I find that he is a good sounding board for me to go to when needing spiritual advice, prayer, or encouragement on the ministry that God has called me to.

2) I have confidence now to step out on my own to witness, to preach, to teach, to disciple, or to minister to those grieving. I do this with the full understanding that if I prepare properly both spiritually and with the skills and talents that I have been given by God, that the Holy Spirit will use me as his vehicle.

3) Something that has also matured over the years is that I think of Paul not as the hero of the 1972 series and a major celebrity, but as my brother in Christ and one of the most important friends in my life. I am not envious of those who see him more often than me because we have mutual respect that involves the more important calling of God to help others find Christ and grow to further the gospel.

4) I do things more honestly today and make fewer excuses for my mistakes, knowing that God has it all under control and loves me just as I am.

5) I respond to the correcting of the Holy Spirit from a biblical point of view and trust the Holy Spirit to make the necessary changes in me for his glory and use in the body of Christ.

6) The first verse that Paul ever shared with me was Romans 1:16, and I attempt to live by that verse. I have seen God honour that stand many times and bless me because of it.

7) I don't feel jealous of those who I was competing with prior to meeting Paul. Many of them have become wealthy by the world's standards, and I am happy for them and still count them as my friends. I will continue to pray for them and be there for them, trusting the eternal destiny to Christ.

I am involved today in the following ways:
1) I still lead or am involved in two discipleship groups challenging men to trust Christ first and not the world.
2) Whenever possible, I try to support Paul if he needs me. He will forever be the one who God used to change the life of my family and myself, giving us a purpose for living with the promise of eternal life.
3) I spend a great deal of time encouraging men to consider Christ and become a part of the discipleship group. I leave the results to the Lord.
4) I have officiated at ten funerals and done more eulogies than I can remember, with the knowledge and understanding about the Holy Spirit as the head of the ministry. This came from the time spent in the word, at church, and with the many men in the many discipleship groups over the years, from the first one with Paul.
5) Today it is much more about sharing Christ in the power of the Holy Spirit rather than in power. It is much more fruitful in His power.
6) I find that I am the go-to guy for many needing help in their spiritual lives. I also find more unbelievers calling me for help when life overtakes them.
7) I fully expect God to use me every day in a new and exciting way. He can use me for anything as long as I trust him.

I plan to be very aggressive the rest of the way to finish well. I am asking God to allow me to push a little harder to win to Christ those who don't know him but whom I love. I will finish, without writing my own book, with a verse that many of my friends know: Cascone 1:1 – "He's on the throne and he's not nervous."

AL BRANDSTATTER – Wealth Management Manager

This weekend, I reflected on not only where my life is today as a result of LeaderImpact Group, but also where my life might have been if not for your spiritual mentoring and friendship.

It was September 2002 when I first attended your group. Truthfully, I had no idea what to expect, and looking back, I can't even imagine the first impression I must have made! I must have seemed so "lost" to you and the other seasoned veterans within the group, but no one ever looked down at me and I was simply accepted with open arms.

At that time, my life resembled the trajectory of Rory McIlroy's pulled tee shot on the tenth at Augusta on that Sunday during the 2011 Masters – which led to one bad shot followed by another and another. I had already purchased a condo and informed both my wife and two young children that I would be moving out. I'll never forget the pain I caused my son when he cried and held on to me, begging me not to leave. Thankfully, when I saw that completed penthouse, even I realized that it was not a home and I was about to abandon my family.

I recall going to church the following Sunday and asking God to help me because I was in way over my head. And on Tuesday, during a previously scheduled golf game with a member at Mississauga Golf and Country Club, I was asked if I would mind having Paul Henderson join our group. "Are you kidding?!" I remember exclaiming. Who knew that your question on the eigth fairway, "How's your spiritual life?" would over time bring that ball deep in the woods back onto the fairway.

And today, my marriage is stronger than ever and my relationship with my kids so very vibrant! But you know better than anyone, it was not easy for me. But through the support, friendship, encouragement, and prayer from the men in the group, I came to have a faith in Christ, and the belief that through God, absolutely nothing is impossible! I'll never forget the first memory assignment you gave me – 1 Corinthians 13:4–8. Before this, I never knew what love truly meant.

And so many other aspects of my life are stronger and better, especially as an advisor and steward of my clients' wealth. Now I come to work knowing that Christ is my boss, and it is the Lord to whom I report.

Last Monday, I was profiled in the National Post *and you called me to tell me you were so proud of me. I can tell you this – your words meant so much more to me than that article!*

Who would believe ten years ago that my 2012 New Year's resolution is to be "single minded" – that is, to have "thought" devoted to Christ, to be joyful regardless of circumstance, and through every circumstance see Christ.

And, Paul, would you have ever thought ten years ago that I would actually be leading more than seventy men at my church, positively influencing those men in how they are as husbands, fathers, employers, employees? It boggles the mind! Last week Father Vid told me that Men's Fraternity is "the defining element at Merciful Redeemer Parish." He went on to say that not only are men's lives being transformed, but also their families and, as a result, the community.

Paul, words cannot express how grateful I am for your support and love! With Christ, you have saved my life!

Now I like to think of my life as McIlroy's ball at Congressional. It occasionally goes awry, but it's on its way to winning the U.S. Open!

I will pray for you and your lovely wife, Eleanor, for the rest of my days.

May God continue to bless you and all your descendants.

LEONARD BUHLER – President, Power to Change

Back in 2001, my wife, Debbie, and I were asked to lead a Campus Crusade for Christ's Power to Change campaign in Manitoba.

Over the course of that campaign, we trained 6,500 people in how to share their faith. We also organized forty-five out-reach events in six regions of the province. When we were booking speakers for those events, we came across the name Paul Henderson. We knew that he was "that guy who scored the goal," so we thought he'd be pretty good. But I didn't actually have a clue who he was.

So we invited Paul to come to Manitoba for a week to speak at some of our events. He promptly called me back and said he was only prepared to give me three days. What a jerk, I thought. This guy works for Campus Crusade, and this is one of their own campaigns. Why would he not come for a full week?

We ended up inviting him anyway. But we hired a charter

airplane, and scheduled Paul to speak at breakfast, at lunch, at coffee, and at dinner. Paul humoured us with our ridiculous schedule, and in the end we managed to pack seven days' worth of speaking engagements into three.

When I first met Paul, I was expecting a typical sports guy – larger than life, a little full of himself. What impressed me about Paul was that yes, he was proud of his sports accomplishments – but he only used his story and his status as a vehicle to tell people about Jesus. I'm originally from the business world, where it's easy to base your whole identity on your money, your success. I knew Paul could easily have done the same thing – based his whole identity on his sports career.

But he didn't. He based it on his relationship with Jesus Christ, and only ever used his sports success to make an impact for Him.

A few years after I met Paul, I became the president of Campus Crusade for Christ, now Power to Change. I had a lot of experience as a business leader but none as a Christian non-profit leader. So I looked around me and tried to find a North Star – another leader I admired, someone I could keep my eyes on and use as a model. Paul Henderson became one of my North Stars because the more I watched him, the more I was impressed.

Three things about Paul really stood out for me. One was his consistency: day in, day out he's followed his purpose statement – "to be a Godly world change agent" – using his life in a significant way for Christ over decades. Another was how he cares for people. Not a week goes by that Paul doesn't phone up to pray for me or leave a great message on my voicemail. On a down day, that's been so encouraging for

*me. In fact, that has had such a huge impact on me that now
I try do the same thing for the people I lead.*

*Finally, what I admire most about Paul is his intimate walk
with Jesus. I don't know very many leaders who have main-
tained such a close relationship with Christ. He's an incredible model, not just for me, but for all Christian leaders – in
ministry and in the marketplace.*

RICK GAETZ – CEO, Vitrain

*Today's kids measure friends in quantities of hundreds and
thousands as defined by the number of friends on their
Facebook page. I grew up in an era when I, too, had many,
many people I would be privileged to call my friends, but I
believe most of us, if lucky enough, have eight or ten people
we would consider lifelong friends: friends who have stood
the test of time and ones that you likely shared the highest
of highs and the lowest of lows.*

*I am privileged to call Paul one of those friends in my life.
Although we have known each other for less than fifteen
years, no one has had a greater impact on me as it relates to
how I live my life. Paul is an evangelical Christian, something
most of us, including myself, are not comfortable with. But
his passion to seek out what is right and what is wrong, all
based on his faith, cannot be argued.*

*The wants are simple . . . he wants us to be better people,
better dads, better husbands, and even better at work. He
wants us to put others ahead of ourselves, something that
doesn't come naturally to many of us. He wants us to compete hard in everything we do, to be the best.*

Paul has had and continues to have an undeniable impact

on my life. My wife would agree. Although I struggle with much of this, I try to be fair but firm in my role as a business leader. I make sure my family is my priority. I am more giving in every way, I am more thoughtful of others, and although many would laugh, I think I am even more patient. Perhaps most remarkably, I am a better golfer as a result of a simple message that he drives home to me every time we play, a message that Paul incorporates in his life every day: "LOOK FORWARD, NOT BACK!"

I have great friends, but no one I know tries to gently nudge people to be better every day as Paul continues to do with me and countless others.

I am proud, privileged, and honoured to call Paul my friend. Above all, Paul shows us that no matter what we are facing in life, we should be grateful for the blessings each day brings.

MIKE HARROWER

Paul's impact on my life has been profound. He has taught me so many things, primarily by modelling admirable attributes in his own life.

I trust him completely for two reasons:

He puts God first, so I never even have to consider whose "agenda" is most important.

Because he "loves his neighbour," I know that he always has my best interests at heart.

By creating this trust he opens my mind and heart to what he can teach me.

So here are a just few of the things I have observed and learned and feebly try to emulate: he is stalwart in his prayer life and I know I am in his prayers. He will call me early in the morning while I am enroute to something he knows that is weighing on my mind and simply say, "Hey, my good buddy, just wanted you to know you were well prayed for this morning!" He encourages in many other ways as well, but just imagine the energy and comfort I get from knowing this formidable "warrior" has my back in this most crucial of undertakings.

After God, his wife comes first. Eleanor is cherished and it is plain for all to see. They way he treats her and talks about her is an example to us all, and I regret that I did not learn and practise this earlier.

He has been steadfast in the pursuit of the purpose that he believes God has for his life. He has poured his life into helping men discover a life-changing faith and has multiplied his efforts by teaching other men to do the same. It is impossible to explain the privilege of witnessing the transformation of just one man's life and subsequently that of his family. There are literally thousands of men who are better husbands, fathers, friends, and contributors to society through Paul. Who of us can say this?

His joy is real and obvious. He will praise God out loud as we walk down some beautiful fairway on a glorious day, but he will also sincerely give thanks for his cancer as it opens new avenues for him to connect with people to explain the joy that is within him. It is not subject to circumstance.

For anybody who doesn't think the above is important, he radically improved my golf swing!

Some would see him as a "man's man"; I see him as an authentic man. He is principled, disciplined, and transparent, yet empathetic, loving, and caring. He is a great mentor and priceless friend!

Simply put, Paul lives one of his favourite sayings: he is "good infection" and I am thankful for his contagion!

DELVIN FLETCHER

Impact and influence is formed in authenticity. Paul is the most authentic person I know. He has learned who he is, he knows what he is about, and he is not afraid to share that with others, both victories and failures.

What I have always admired is that he has chosen to do most of this in the unpublished setting of an early morning, a boardroom table, ten or twelve men, no cameras, no reporters.

I have had the privilege of listening to the public Paul, participating in some of those early mornings, and sharing a friendship at a more personal level. I see the same man in each of those settings, a consistency these days that is perhaps more rare than we realize. And it causes me to want that for my life as well.

GREGG FERRIS

Paul's influence has enabled me to live my life in a more peaceful way, in part by recognizing the importance of "people" in my life.

His teachings, using everyday examples (often in humorous ways), assisted me in stepping back and recognizing the "bigger" picture of life, to concentrate on the blessings I have and the importance of listening and helping others.

Thank you, Paul.

PAUL WEST

Engaging. Excited. Encouraging. Positive. Challenging. Brutally honest.

Every so often you meet a man and you say, "I want to be more like that."

Paul Henderson is that man for me.

Paul has helped me to see the joy of the Christian life again. He is helping me to grow in character.

He is helping me to have a more positive approach to the Christian life (which can be a difficult walk sometimes).

Perhaps most importantly, Paul is guiding me toward a deeper level of Bible study, helping me to see the value and joy of time spent in God's word.

HAROLD PERCY

Paul Henderson has had a huge influence on my life in many ways.

Paul's passionate commitment to Jesus and his dedication and discipline in taking his relationship with Jesus deeper and deeper has been a wonderful model to me of a Christian life well lived. His example in this has been an inspiration to me and an encouragement to go deeper in my own relationship with Jesus than I otherwise might have.

I also love and have benefited from his passion to help others go deeper, stay focused, and finish well.

Paul's exuberant joy in simply living his life is contagious. He has an almost childlike enthusiasm for living fully – enjoying a game of golf or a nice meal or a good conversation or a funny joke – that lifts everyone around him to a higher level and a deeper appreciation for the simple joys of life. Paul has shown me what it means to live more fully by simply being alive to the present moment and enjoying what is happening.

I have been impressed with and helped by Paul's emphasis in his ministry on encouraging and challenging men to love their wives well and to show this love to them every day. He himself sets a wonderful example in this, as he does in his challenges to men to step up and be the spiritual leaders in their homes.

Paul is extremely wise and has given me excellent counsel on diverse issues over the years.

Maybe most of all, Paul knows what it means to be a true and loyal friend, in good times and in bad. We have had a lot of good laughs together and enjoyed many good times, but my deepest appreciation of him as a friend and guide has to do with the many occasions he shared my tears as I was going through difficult times.

It is hard to capture all this in just a few words, but it is certainly true that Paul is one of the few men one meets in life for whom the description "great" is totally appropriate.

RIC SINGOR

The year was 1998 and life was completely out of balance. Work was consuming me; my family and church were definitely in second place. I was tired out. A friend gave me an invitation to listen to Paul speak at a local breakfast meeting. I went more out of a desire to please him than attend another meeting.

Paul shared that it wasn't until he became a Christian that he found his inner peace. I recommitted my life to Christ that morning and refocused my life's priorities. The changes in me personally were phenomenal. My frustrations subsided knowing God was designing my life, not me. Paul taught me that the answers to life's questions were available through reading God's word and prayer.

Paul is responsible for the men's groups that meet in Muskoka each week. These groups have become instrumental in keeping me focused on what I learned from Paul that morning.

I will be forever indebted to Paul for the work he does sharing his personal life story, his love for Christ, and the impact that he has had on my life.

RON ELLIS ON PAUL'S SPIRITUAL LIFE

It looked for a while that Paul was going to stay in the United States, but some things happened that he's talked about in this book that prevented that. He decided to come back to Canada, and we renewed our relationship right away. We retired at around the same time, we had played together as well, so it only figured that we would remain friends when our playing days were over, especially when he came back. The hockey wasn't what was holding us together this time, however; it was our commitment to becoming Christians.

We became even closer as friends during this time, as we both came to know the Lord. He really helped me in my spiritual journey, and our friendship deepened even more. I have to be honest, we don't see each other as often as we did, but every time we are together, we just pick up where we left off, which is a true indication of friendship. I was there for him when he started his ministry and supported him in every *way I could, and he's been very supportive of what I have been doing over the years as well. If either one of us needed anything, I know that it would just take a short phone call and the other one would be there in a heartbeat. He has been a great friend to me, and what he's done since he stopped playing has really helped define his great life. He has helped so many people along the way.*

CHAPTER FIFTEEN

THOSE KIND WORDS IN THE PREVIOUS CHAPTER MEAN more to me than anyone could ever imagine. Life is short, and knowing that you have touched people and made their lives better, and knowing that there are so many people who would support you as well, is a tremendous source of comfort and satisfaction to me.

We really do not know how long we have, as the length of our lives is not determined by us. This is why we should try to enjoy every day of our lives as we are living them, and try to help as many people as we can along our journey. We never know what is in store for us.

I sure never suspected that getting cancer was in store for me.

A couple of years ago, right around the time of Eleanor and my forty-seventh wedding anniversary (on November 9, 2009), I went in for my annual checkup. I was feeling fit and healthy and expected it would just be another routine exam.

As part of the checkup, an ultrasound was done on my stomach. I knew the technician who was performing the procedure very well, and as she was doing the test, she became really quiet while I lay there. She didn't say anything, but I knew she was plotting growths on the screen. I could just tell.

It takes a while to get the results back, but when I went home, I let Eleanor know that I suspected something was up.

"I think I'm in trouble," I told her directly.

We had booked a hotel room for a Friday night about two weeks later as part of our anniversary plans, and just as we were checking into the hotel my doctor called me with the news.

It turned out I was right: I was in trouble.

"We have the results," he said to me matter-of-factly, "and it definitely looks like you have cancer."

Those words hit me like a hard punch right in the stomach. *I had cancer.*

After I hung up, I turned to the woman who had been with me through thick and thin for close to five decades and said simply, "I have cancer."

The Lord moves in mysterious ways, and often our faith is challenged in ways we cannot imagine until we face those ways. I was facing a real battle now, especially at sixty-six years of age.

We had the diagnosis confirmed with a biopsy at the Mayo Clinic, and confirmed again in hospitals in Boston and Toronto. It turned out all three places agreed that I had chronic lymphocytic leukemia and that it was in my abdomen, my lymph nodes, my chest, and my blood.

My oncologist spelled it out for me in no uncertain terms.

"The bad news is, there is no known cure," he told me. "However, what we have here is slow-moving cancer, and that is good news.

"With this cancer, we'll wait until you are in too much pain, or you face a lot of weight loss, or there is too much growth, before we start chemotherapy."

I was told that 80 percent of the people who are treated can recover and have good health for five years, and it would generally come back again after that. I spent several months learning about cancer and what I might do to slow it down, and possibly even get rid of it. I started taking supplements, started following a very strict diet, and really started working out a great deal to help my immune system fight off this disease. I would be checked out every three months, I was told, and if all went well I'd have perhaps a year, or maybe a year and a half, before undergoing the chemo. Just before I got my diagnosis, my longtime friend and mentor John Bradford found out that he was battling pancreatic cancer. When you compare what I had to his form of cancer, I was the one better off.

I called him and told him, "Bradford, this following you around has gone on long enough. Now I'm following your having cancer!"

It was devastating news – don't get me wrong. All I knew was that I had to deal with it. I believe there is a reason for everything that happens to you in your life, even when there is no understanding.

Having cancer has given me a new platform to speak to people from. Now I wasn't just Paul Henderson, the guy who scored the Goal of the Century; I was Paul Henderson the hockey player who had cancer. In addition to wanting to talk to me about the goal, they would now ask me, "How are you doing?" and that would give me an opportunity to speak to them about how my faith was helping me through this, backing up the beliefs I have had all along.

John had mentored me since 1976, and I had memorized so much scripture by this time that it really helped me deal with all this. The comforting words of the Bible rang so true to me during this time. And the Lord assures us that He will help us through everything.

Jesus is speaking to His best friends, His apostles, in John 16:33, when he says, "I have told you these things, so that in Me you may have peace. In this world you *will* have trouble. But take heart! I have overcome the world." Note that it says you *will* have trouble – no maybes! There is no such thing as a trouble-free life, but we will find help and guidance from Him at all times.

At no time after getting the diagnosis was I fearful, or even suffering any angst. It amazes me even now that I have been so much at peace with all this. I don't believe that God gave me cancer, but He knows I have it. And I wouldn't have it if He didn't think I could handle it.

I even came to be able to thank the Lord that I had cancer, as it gave me an intimacy with Him that wouldn't have been possible without it. When you have no fear or angst, it really is amazing how well you can live each day.

Of course it is difficult. But I do what anyone should do, and that is ask the Lord for His help every morning and take one day at a time. You certainly learn to differentiate the trivial from the important very quickly when you have cancer.

I firmly believe that the Lord wants you to try to enjoy life every day. On this side of heaven there are no answers as to why something like this happens to us. The Bible teaches us to walk by faith, not by sight, and we have to have trust in Him, not ourselves. I trust in the Lord.

This struggle has not been easy. Although the cancer is moving slowly, every day gets a little worse. The biggest challenge of the past two years has been in keeping weight on, the exact opposite problem a lot of people have, I know! But I've managed, even though I've lost some weight in the last two years.

We all need a reason to get up in the morning and to stay up. My reason is that I have dedicated my life 100 percent to the Lord since 1975 and that has motivated me ever since. I lived the first thirty-two years of my life without a spiritual dimension, so I have seen both sides of the equation. I now know to trust in Him and leave it to Him to decide how this plays out.

I still keep busy and I'm very active. I have no desire to ever retire from what I am doing. I'm always on the go, even since the diagnosis, and still do numerous speaking engagements. I have spoken hundreds of times about my beliefs all over the world. And I have been honoured to speak about my faith to whomever wishes to hear me.

I want to finish well. I want to finish my life well in every way. I still have goals, things to do, and I continue speaking about my faith when the opportunities come along.

I didn't start off well, as I didn't become a Christian until I was thirty-two. But for more than half my life now I have dedicated myself to the Lord, and whatever His plans for me are the rest of the way are okay by me.

Hey, look, this time we call life here on earth is not the game. This is just a blip for us really – we are built for eternity. When you look at your life on earth in that context, you realize this is just a very brief period of time, no matter how long you may live. Everyone dies eventually; it is a part of our lives here on earth. So my viewpoint is: why should any of us fear the inevitable?

I don't know how much longer I have, but I do know this about my life here on earth:

I want to finish well in every way . . . and I want to hear the words "Well done, good and faithful servant" when I see Jesus.

CHAPTER SIXTEEN

WE'VE HAD A CHANCE TO RELIVE SOME OF THE GREAT
memories of the 1972 Summit Series thanks to the Henderson
Jersey Homecoming Tour, sponsored by SmartCentres. Our
travels have taken us across this great country of ours, and
it's been a lot of fun.

The jersey I wore in Moscow was bought by Mitch
Goldhar, the owner of SmartCentres, for $1.275 million. It
was a tremendous gesture on his part; he wanted Canadians
to be able to relive the experience of the series and he wanted
to educate those people not alive in 1972 about it as well.

In the official release after he purchased the jersey through
Classic Auctions, Goldhar was very flattering toward me
and what the 1972 Canada–Russia series meant to all
Canadians.

"I am pleased and proud to bring this important piece of
Canadian history home," he said. "As a lifelong hockey fan,
I know what Paul Henderson's winning goal against the
Russians in 1972 meant to all Canadians."

I was very pleased that the jersey was brought home to Canada. I had given the jersey to our Team Canada trainer, Joe Sgro, as a gift, and he eventually sold it to someone in the United States. The owner decided to put it up for auction through Classic Auctions, and Mitch Goldhar's bid was the winning one. It was truly humbling to see the level of interest that auction generated – not to mention the incredible amount of money it fetched.

Recently, the *Guinness Book of World Records* declared that it was the highest amount ever paid for a hockey jersey, and it may be the highest amount ever paid for any sports jersey. And by Mitch Goldhar buying it, it gave us a chance to put together this Henderson Jersey Homecoming Tour.

I made it to a lot of the cities and towns across the country to meet people and hear their stories, and that has been a lot of fun. I dropped the puck at several NHL games and did numerous radio and television interviews to promote the tour. I have to say, it's been really heartwarming. When you walk out onto the ice and get a standing ovation from the fans after all these years, it's something pretty special. To be able to travel to all those cities and get that close to the game once again is tremendous. I've had a chance to talk with coaches and reminisce. In Ottawa, when I dropped the puck just before the start of the game, Senators captain Daniel Alfredsson came up to me and said it was a great pleasure to meet me, a very nice gesture on his part. How can you not feel good about that?

Eleanor travelled with me on some of these stops, and that makes everything extra-special, as we have been a team through all this – and she always asks me, "How does it feel when you walk out on the ice and hear those cheers. Does it bring back the memories?"

It sure does. It's very satisfying to be appreciated and remembered like that. And when you think that maybe 60 to 70 percent of people in the building weren't even born when The Goal was scored, it makes you realize that hockey is in our DNA in this country. We love the game like no other country in the world.

I found that out once again when I helped write a book last year called *How Hockey Defines Canada,* and the title is very appropriate, I think. Hockey really does define our great country, and I see proof of that whenever I travel in Canada.

I have embraced this recognition. I have enjoyed it – I always have, but maybe we get even more nostalgic as we get older, so it means more. I have never shied away from the publicity that this goal has brought to me, and I still enjoy sharing the moment with people after all these years.

The Henderson Jersey Homecoming Tour was housed in a forty-eight-foot trailer with double wide-outs that we took around the country, making 104 stops from the time we opened up in Lucknow, my hometown, on my birthday – January 28, 2011 – to our last stop in Georgetown, Ontario, on February 18, 2012. At several stops along the way, other players associated with the series were also on hand, including guys like Yvan Cournoyer for the stops in Quebec, Ron Ellis, Dennis Hull, and even Vladislav Tretiak, who did his best to stop us from winning that series back in 1972.

We started the tour in my hometown of Lucknow and went to Kincardine and Goderich, my old stomping grounds, and then to every province in the country. The trailer was filled with rare Canadian hockey memorabilia and several screens showing highlights from the series and interviews with the players; interactive games and activities; and, of course, the jersey I wore to score the Goal of the Century in Moscow. The fans came out in great numbers wherever we were, and there were always a lot of pictures taken and stories told. The trailer was usually open for five hours at each stop, and I would talk to the crowd and answer questions and then take hundreds of pictures with people and the sweater.

And before anyone asks, no, I do not get tired of hearing the stories of where people were when the goal was scored – even after forty years! And I get new stories all the time. I wonder sometimes how I could still hear one I haven't heard before, but I do, from right across the country. Recently, I found out that several people were fired from their jobs for taking time off to watch the game in the middle of the day! I know the country was engulfed in hockey fever, but I guess there was the odd boss out there who just didn't get it. But even though it cost them their jobs, the people who told me that story all don't regret it for a single minute. Wow, now THOSE are hockey fans!

I met two women who told me they were university students in Windsor at the time, and they just decided they had to find a way to get to Russia to see the games there, even with the cost of going and missing classes. They told me they weren't going to miss it, no matter what. "For some reason we just had to do this," one told me.

It really was a special time, and a unique thing that we won't see again in our lifetimes. It really was us versus them, our way of life versus theirs. Yes, there have been a lot of great moments in hockey in this country and a lot of accomplishments, but it is called the Goal of the Century and we were the Team of the Century.

Sidney Crosby's goal was huge for Canada at the 2010 Vancouver Olympics, and Mario Lemieux's goal at the Canada Cup in 1987 was beautiful to watch. I went nuts cheering for both of those goals and felt proud to be a Canadian when they both went in. But our 1972 Canada–Russia series was a unique, once-in-a-lifetime event that we'll never see again, and I was fortunate to have played a part in it, as I have been riding that one goal for forty years!

With two grandchildren in Oakville playing minor hockey, Eleanor and I see more kids' hockey than we do NHL games, for obvious reasons. I still enjoy getting down to the Air Canada Centre the odd time to see the Maple Leafs, and when I do watch, I have to say that the product put out by the National Hockey League today is, by and large, pretty good.

The game is so quick and fast now. The transition game most teams have is terrific – they get the puck out of their own end so fast and in a couple of seconds it's up the ice, just like that. Like most fans, I don't like teams that play the trap, but when the game is opened up, it really is great to watch. There is incredible parity in the NHL because of the salary cap, which is a good thing – there are always two or three or four teams trying to make the playoffs on the last night of the season, and that makes it very exciting for the fans. There are no dynasties anymore in the NHL, and so many teams have a shot at the Stanley Cup.

If you asked me to pick a Stanley Cup winner, I'd have to pick five or six teams – maybe more – before I felt comfortable that I had the winner. In 2011, not many predicted the Boston Bruins would win the Stanley Cup, but the reality is, they did it. There is no prohibitive favourite anymore, and all in all, that is a good thing for the NHL. It gives hope to a lot of hockey fans that their team's turn might come one day.

In my heart, I am still a Leafs fan. As somebody who lives in Mississauga, I'd like nothing more than to see the Toronto Maple Leafs win the Stanley Cup someday. Now wouldn't that be something to see!

I like their team speed now. In the 2011–12 season, they had a competitive team, and most nights were really fast, which is why I enjoy going to the games these days. It looks like the team is enjoying playing and they have each other's backs. I think the Leafs have a lot of character people and a lot of skill, but I just wish they could learn how to win more often, as once again they missed the playoffs.

I live in Canada and I'm an alumnus of the Maple Leafs organization, so I'm going to cheer them on. I do hope that one day they'll come through for all their great fans across the country. I'd like nothing more.

As I said earlier, Maple Leaf Gardens is a very special place to me, and now it may be coming back into vogue again.

The Gardens has recently been redeveloped, with a Loblaws grocery store on the main floor and athletic facilities for Ryerson University, including a hockey arena, due to open in the fall of 2012. I think it's fantastic, I really do.

The Gardens has a special place in my heart and I have great memories of it, stretching back to when I was a kid and went there for the first time. Of course, playing in the building was special, but it was always a classy place to be, and as it would have been for so many other youngsters, my first trip there was very special.

We were living in Lucknow and I was twelve years old. We had a coach who knew Bobby Bauer, the former Boston Bruin, who had arranged for us to get tickets for a game in Toronto, between the Leafs and the Bruins. Well, six of us jammed into a car and off we went for the three-hour drive to Toronto. It's quite a drive even today, and this was before Highway 401 opened, so it was a major trip for some kids and their coach, to be sure.

When we set foot in Maple Leaf Gardens, I swear, our eyes were as wide as saucers! Our tickets were in the second row from the top of the greys, so we couldn't have been farther away from the play, but we loved every minute of it. Don't ask me who won the game because it was so long ago now I don't remember the details, but I never slept a minute on the long drive back home. We were still so excited afterwards that we talked about that trip for days.

There are so many great memories associated with the Gardens, and I was fortunate to be a part of many of them as a player *and* as a fan. I was at the Muhammad Ali–George Chuvalo fight, for instance.

The electricity in the building that night was unbelievable. And the fact that the fight was held in such a historic building made it all the more amazing to me. It was just a great battle to see in person. You really had a sense that you were seeing history in the making that night.

The Air Canada Centre is a terrific building, but anyone with memories of Maple Leaf Gardens was saddened to see it close and sit for so long with nothing happening inside it.

I'm really, really glad to see it open again and being used, at least in part, as a hockey arena once again.

It would be impossible to duplicate the 1972 Canada–Russia series just because of the kind of event it was. It really was a once-in-a-lifetime experience. But that doesn't mean international hockey isn't just as great as ever.

I love international hockey today mostly because it gives players a chance to represent their country. Hockey is in our blood in Canada, and players always want to prove that Canada is the best hockey country in the world. It is a source of pride when you get a chance to wear the maple leaf on your jersey.

Other countries are getting better all the time, though. We were surprised by the strength of the Russians in 1972, but there are no surprises anymore in international hockey. The other countries we play all have tremendous pride too, and would love nothing better than to knock Canada off the pedestal.

I thought the hockey at the last few world junior tournaments was as good as I've ever seen, and the Olympics are the same. There is great parity in international hockey now among the top teams, and while that might be tough for some Canadians to take, it's good for the growth of the game overall.

In 1972, we had our eyes opened to just how good the skill level was outside of Canada when we played the Russians. Now we see it all the time. The athletes of today are so much better conditioned and so much better prepared from such a young age – kids nine and ten and eleven years old basically play pro-style schedules now – and the skill level in Canada and around the world is greatly improved as a result.

I love to watch Canada in international competition any time. It's still our game, and having to answer the challenge from countries that have improved so much over the years just makes us that much better.

There isn't a more polarizing debate in hockey than the subject of fighting. There are those who think fighting is a part of hockey and those who think it has no part in the game.

Simply put, I don't think the game of hockey needs fighting anymore. I think we're past that now because the game has changed so much in so many ways over the years.

For one thing, it's such a fast game now. And think about when the best hockey anywhere is played: in the Stanley Cup playoffs and the Olympics. Now think about how the game is played during these events. There is hardly any fighting in the playoffs and none in the Olympics because it's not needed.

It takes away from the game, in my mind, and besides, players today are just too big and too strong. I'm really afraid somebody is going to get killed out there.

Staged fighting in particular just drives me crazy. What's the point of that – a staged fight that everybody can see coming? Those kinds of fights are definitely not necessary.

We also have to ask, seriously, just how many blows to the head players can take before it affects them psychologically. We've seen how players who have been enforcers all their careers have turned out. Some of these guys have admitted that they were up all night, worried to death, knowing that they would have to fight the next night and how that would go. During my career, I'd never thought of it from that viewpoint – I just looked forward to playing. But it must have been really tough on some players, especially as they got older. To hear that guys were losing sleep over whom they had to fight next – well, life is just too short for that kind of stuff.

I have always believed that the game will police itself, and I think there is still accountability within the game without the need for fighting. A lot of young kids are quitting the game because the idea of fighting is just not in their makeup, and that is a real shame. I would hate for my grandchildren to have to fight just to play the game of hockey, so why would I wish that burden on somebody else's grandchildren?

We teach our children that they don't have to fight in life to be men, and hopefully we are evolving in a lot of ways on that front. The defenders of fighting in hockey will say that it's always been a part of the game and therefore it should always be. I say no to that. There is no excuse anymore to keep fighting in the game of hockey. We don't need it. It's time to get beyond that mentality.

Mainly because of that goal I scored in Moscow forty years ago, I understand what fame is. There is both good and bad in fame and I have accepted it all.

But that fame and my achievement in hockey have not been enough to get me into the Hockey Hall of Fame.

The 1972 Summit Series team has been recognized and honoured throughout the hockey world, including inside the Hockey Hall of Fame. Heck, being named the Team of the Century is certainly getting recognized. None of us, myself included, suffer for a lack of recognition in this great country of ours. We were national heroes when we returned from the

Soviet Union and we are still recognized and saluted wherever we go for the achievement. The twenty-fifth-anniversary celebrations in 1997 were tremendous, and the upcoming fortieth anniversary promises to be the biggest yet. We all love the attention, even after all these years.

Wherever I go across the country, I guess nine out of every ten people tell me I should be in the Hockey Hall of Fame. It is flattering to me that people would think that way and let me know how much they support me. I appreciate their thoughts, I really do. But let me state here, clearly, for the record, once and for all: I have no problem with not being in the Hockey Hall of Fame.

The Hall has a selection committee, and that committee has its criteria. I understand that. I also understand that if it were not for the 1972 series and what I did, I wouldn't even merit consideration for the Hockey Hall of Fame. I was a good NHL player, but I don't have the numbers or the All-Star status or major trophy wins to be a candidate. I feel there are many retired players more deserving than me who still haven't been inducted.

I had a month for the ages, that's for sure, but the Hockey Hall of Fame selection committee criteria is all about great *careers*. Don't take that to mean that I don't appreciate all the support, or that I am not proud of the career I had in the game. I'm still very proud of my NHL accomplishments. I'm especially proud to have played on two top lines, with Norm Ullman and Bruce MacGregor in Detroit, and then with Norm and Ron Ellis in Toronto.

I thought the Henderson–Ullman–Ellis line was as good as any in the NHL. We were defensively responsible and we could play any style and play with any forward unit in the league. I get great satisfaction in knowing that, and in the way we all contributed. While we were playing together in Toronto, Ellis had 152 goals and 147 assists, Ullman scored 152 and had 267 assists – he was always the playmaker! – and I had 157 goals and 150 assists. How is that for consistency and sharing the wealth!

There was one season where I led the league in game-winning goals with nine out of the twenty-two goals I scored overall. I was an opportunist in that sense, and I really tried to score important goals. I think everybody wants to be on the ice at key times, but I really thrived on that during my entire career, not just in Russia.

I always enjoyed when the pressure was on, and I didn't shrink away from those situations. I also played with some great linemates who felt the same way, and that made it a lot easier to succeed in those situations as well.

It was tough playing on some teams that didn't win, but any player would feel the same way about that. The Toronto teams I played on were generally older and, thanks to Harold Ballard, were generally in disarray. Nobody was going to win any championships in that situation.

I thought we had a great team in Detroit before I got traded to the Leafs. We seemed to be really close to winning the Cup, but then Doug Barkley lost an eye, Marcel Pronovost got traded, and Bill Gadsby retired. We just couldn't get over those losses, but I thought we really had a chance to do something special there.

But there are really no regrets from that standpoint either. I had a long career, I made some decent money, and I had the kind of life that the vast majority of people in the world would be very envious of.

Thanks to September 1972, I had lots of fame too! And I had my time in the spotlight, which gave me recognition and a platform in this country to do the work I have been doing with my ministry for many years now, to an extent that wouldn't have been possible without that recognition.

Every player would love to be in the Hockey Hall of Fame, but the fact that I'm not seems to bother other people a lot more than it bothers me. The bottom line is, I've had a wonderful life and career in hockey that I am very proud of. I've been a very fortunate guy.

Even after forty years, the 1972 Summit Series is still receiving accolades for what it meant to the game of hockey.

The International Ice Hockey Federation (IIHF) recently introduced an IIHF Milestone Award, to be granted periodically "to a team or teams that have made a significant contribution to international ice hockey or had a defining impact on the development of the game." The council decided that the first such honour would go to the teams of the 1972 Summit Series.

The timing of this first award was intended to help mark the forty-year anniversary of the series, and it really is quite an honour for all of us to receive, especially after all these years.

IIHF president Rene Fasel was gracious in his comments as he outlined the rationale for the award: "The IIHF has honoured individuals since 1997 with inductions to the IIHF Hall of Fame, but we felt we were missing an award which recognized great events, great teams, or defining moments which have shaped our game. This is why we introduced this new award, and the council felt it was appropriate that the historic 1972 Summit Series would receive the inaugural honour."

The award was presented as part of the IIHF Hall of Fame induction ceremony on May 20, 2012, in Helsinki, Finland, on the day of the gold medal game of the seventy-sixth IIHF Ice Hockey World Championship. In 1972, Canada was sitting on the sidelines as far as international hockey went, so when you consider how much has happened since then – with Canada earning both respect and gold medals at the Winter Olympics, world championships, and world junior championships – the tournament seems to be a perfect setting for the teams of the Summit Series to be remembered.

My good feelings about our accomplishment in Moscow only get deeper as the years go on. But as I watch today's players at the Air Canada Centre, it is really hard to believe how time sure flies, especially as you get older.

And my goodness, to think that the fortieth anniversary of that series is upon us! Now where did that time go? It certainly is a perfect time for reflection and looking back, that's for sure.

Eleanor and I will look in the mirror some days and say, "Who are those people?" We've got a lot more wrinkles, and sometimes it does make you wonder where the years have gone. I'm sure my teammates think the same thing some days, although we really have been blessed. In those forty years we've only lost three players and one coach from Team Canada '72: Bill Goldsworthy, Gary Bergman, and Rick Martin, along with assistant coach John Ferguson. But time catches up with all of us, and several of us are battling cancer. We know this fortieth anniversary is likely our last hurrah, so we're all looking forward to it.

There really is a certain amount of luck that comes with just being around as long as we've all been, and having the opportunity to celebrate an event forty years after it ends. When you look back and see all that we have survived, from injuries to illness to other challenges, and you realize that we've all made it and had such great lives, you just say "Wow!" to yourself.

When you are young, you think you are immortal. You get a real sense of appreciation for everything in life as you get older, as you realize just how lucky you have been in your life, even just to have played in the NHL for as long as you did.

The Goal in 1972 was an epic moment. We knew that then, but we know that even more so today. I certainly cherish it more today, that's for sure. It is such a thrill even to be able to share it with my grandchildren, who are so proud of me for the accomplishment. It's another generation being exposed to what happened, and when I saw all the young people walking through the Henderson Jersey Homecoming Trailer, well, it really made an old man feel good.

But as you reflect back on your life, it's the friendships and relationships that really matter the most, isn't it? That is true of all of us. It's not how much money you have made, it's how many friends you have made over the years that is the important thing.

Look, whenever there's a fire in a house and people have to leave in a hurry, what's the first thing they grab? The pictures. That says a lot about what is really important to people, doesn't it?

As I get closer to the end of my journey, I'm so fortunate to be able to spend my life now doing what I want to do with it. Eleanor and I spend so much time together travelling and enjoying our family (and especially watching the grandchildren play hockey now as the younger generation takes to the ice!), and we're always together – well, except for golf, which is my thing alone – but we do just about everything else together, which is really wonderful. I love my work and I'll continue to do that until I can't do it anymore. That shows how much I love what I've been able to do for so many years now.

This – our lives on earth – is not the game. It's just the warm-up. Christ wants us to get to know Him. I believe there is an eternity ahead of us where we will really get to know God intimately, and what He has prepared for us there will absolutely blow us all away. All the hassles, problems, tragedies, failures, and bad breaks that we have had will never even be thought of. Thoughts of heaven and of eternity make living with cancer here on earth seem very insignificant.

The Bible says in many places that we should not fear, not worry, not even be anxious about anything, and that is how I try to live every day. When we are able to do that, there is nothing that happens to us that we cannot handle with God's help.

As the thirty-fourth Psalm says, "I sought the Lord, and He heard me, and delivered me from all my fears."

I have a simple mantra now: "Start small. Go deep. Think big. Finish well." That is the way that I try to live my life spiritually every single day.

The Goal of My Life was scored on September 28, 1972, in Moscow. It was such a fantastic moment for me and for all Canadians, and I am so thankful for it. I will cherish it forever.

But to live my life the way I have since I became a Christian, to live a life that pleases Him, to be His Godly world change agent – that is the real Goal of My Life. And I thank God that I've been able to pursue that goal for so long.

Timeline

January 28, 1943 Born in Kincardine, Ontario, but raised mostly in Lucknow, Ontario, when his family moved there.

1958 Scores 18 goals in a single game while playing for Lucknow, gaining the attention of NHL scouts.

1959–60 Joins the Goderich Sailors of the Western Ontario Junior B Hockey League after signing with the Detroit Red Wings organization. The Sailors finish second in the league with a 22–8 record (44 points), losing to the fourth-place Sarnia Legionnaires 3–1 (with 2 ties) in the WOJBHL semifinals.

1960–61 Joins the Hamilton Red Wings of the Ontario Hockey Association Junior A league. Accumulates a goal and 3 assists in 30 regular-season games, adding a goal and an assist in 12 playoff games. Team finishes third in the seven-team loop, with a record of 22–19–7.

1961–62 In his second season with Hamilton, Paul finishes fourth in team scoring with 24 goals and 19 assists for 43 points in 50 regular-season games. The team places second among 6 teams in the OHA Provincial Junior A league, amassing a record of 32–12–6. Paul scores 4 goals and 6 assists for 10 points in 10 playoff games as Hamilton defeats the St. Catharines Teepees and Niagara Falls Flyers to claim the OHA championship. The Red Wings then defeat the Toronto St. Michael's Majors to win the all-Ontario title, then the Quebec Citadelles to become the champions of Eastern Canada. They receive the George Richardson Memorial Trophy and a berth in the Memorial Cup final. They defeat the western champions, the Edmonton Oil Kings, 4–1 in the best-of-seven series, to win the Memorial Cup for the first time. In 14 games against St. Mike's, Quebec, and Edmonton, Paul scores 7 goals and adds 7 assists for 14 points.

1962–63 Paul enjoys his best junior season, leading the OHA with 49 goals in 48 games, while adding 27 assists for 76 points. Is awarded the Red Tilson Trophy as the OHA Junior A league's most outstanding player. Registers 2 goals in 3 playoff games. Also makes his NHL debut as a call-up for 2 games with the Detroit Red Wings. Records no points but spends 9 minutes in the penalty box.

1963–64 Turns pro and plays 38 games with the
Pittsburgh Hornets of the American Hockey
League, Detroit's farm team, where he registers
10 goals and 14 assists for 24 points. He is
called up to the Red Wings just after Christmas
and scores 3 goals and 3 assists in 32 games. In
14 playoff games with Detroit, he notches 2
goals and 3 assists as the Red Wings are
defeated by the Toronto Maple Leafs (4–3) in
the Stanley Cup finals. He will remain with the
Red Wings until March 1968.

1964–65 Plays his first full NHL season, appearing in all
70 regular-season games, with 8 goals and 13
assists for 21 points. Records 2 assists in 7
playoff games as the Red Wings are eliminated
by the Chicago Blackhawks (4–3) in the opening
round of the Stanley Cup playoffs.

1965–66 Has his first 20-goal season in the NHL, with
22 goals and 24 assists for 46 points in 69
regular-season games. Nine of the 22 goals are
game-winners, tops among NHL scorers.
Scores 3 goals and adds 3 assists for 6 points
in 12 playoff games as the Red Wings defeat
Chicago in the first round but lose to the
Montreal Canadiens (4–2) in the Stanley Cup
finals.

1966–67 Chest, groin, and knee injuries as well as breathing problems limit Paul to 46 regular-season

games. He scores 21 goals and 19 assists for 40 points. (His average of .46 goals per game is third-best in the NHL.) Red Wings finish fifth, missing the playoffs by 14 points.

1967–68 Puts up 13 goals and 20 assists for 33 points in 50 regular-season games with the Red Wings before being traded, with Norm Ullman and Floyd Smith, to the Toronto Maple Leafs in exchange for Frank Mahovlich, Garry Unger, Pete Stemkowski, and the NHL rights to Carl Brewer on March 3, 1968. He notches 5 goals and 6 assists for 11 points in 13 regular-season games with the Maple Leafs. Leafs finish fifth in the East Division, missing the playoffs by four points.

1968–69 In his first full season with the Maple Leafs, Paul sets new career highs in goals (27), assists (32), and points (59) in 74 regular-season games. Leafs finish fourth in the East (fifth overall) but are swept 4 straight in the first round by the Boston Bruins. Paul records 1 assist in the 4 games.

1969–70 Despite a groin injury, Paul records his fourth 20-goal season in the NHL, with 20 goals and 22 assists for 42 points in 67 regular-season games. Under new coach John McLellan, Toronto finishes sixth in the East and fails to qualify for the playoffs.

1970–71 Scores 30 goals for the first time (his fifth season with at least 20), adding 30 assists for a career-high 60 points in 72 regular-season games. Leafs finish fourth in the East (sixth overall) and are defeated by the New York Rangers (4–2) in the Stanley Cup quarter-finals. Paul scores 5 goals and adds an assist in 6 playoff games. Scores the winning goal in both of Toronto's victories in the series.

1971–72 Scores a career-high 38 goals, and adds 19 assists for 57 points in 73 regular-season games. Ranks tenth in the NHL in goals, and fourth in shooting percentage (19.9 percent). Maple Leafs finish fourth in the East, sixth overall. Meet the Boston Bruins in the quarter-finals and are defeated 4–1. Paul scores a goal and two assists in the series.

January 25, 1972 Plays in the twenty-fifth NHL All-Star Game in Bloomington, Minnesota, on January 25. Wears number 17 for the East Division team (his familiar number 19 was assigned to Jean Ratelle of the New York Rangers). The East defeats the West 3–2 before a crowd of 15,423. 21 of the 38 players who take part in the game will be on the roster of Team Canada 1972.

September 1972 Henderson achieves hockey fame in Canada after scoring the game-winning goals in the final three games of the eight-game Summit Series, leading Canada to a thrilling victory. He finishes the tournament with 7 goals and 3 assists for 10 points in 8 games played. The goal in the last game was recently declared the greatest sports moment of the twentieth century, and Team Canada '72 was voted the Team of the Century.

1972–73 Limited by injuries to 40 regular-season games, scores 18 goals and 16 assists. Toronto finishes sixth in the East Division (thirteenth among 16 teams) and fails to qualify for the playoffs.

January 30, 1973 Played in the twenty-sixth NHL All-Star Game for the East Division All-Stars. Wearing number 21, Henderson gives the East a 3–1 lead at 19:12 of the second period on a goal assisted by Phil Esposito and Ken Hodge. The East wins 5–4 before 16,986 at Madison Square Garden in New York.

1973–74 Seventh 20-goal season for Paul Henderson: 24 goals and 31 assists for 55 points in 69 regular-season games. Leafs rebound to fourth place in the East (and sixth overall), but are swept 4 straight by Boston in the quarter-finals. In the 4 games, Paul records 2 assists.

1974 Leaves the Toronto Maple Leafs and the NHL, joining the Toronto Toros of the rival WHA.

September 1974 Participates in the 1974 Summit Series. This time, the Russians win, taking 4 of the 8 games. Team Canada, represented by the WHA's top players, wins just 1 game, and the other 3 are played to a draw. Henderson plays in 7 games, scoring 2 goals and 1 assist for three points.

1974–75 Scores 30 goals and 33 assists in 58 regular-season games with the Toros, averaging better than a point a game. Toros' record of 43–33–2 ranks them second in the WHA Canadian Division (fifth overall out of 14 teams). A season-ending knee injury keeps Paul out of the playoffs, in which the Toros lose 4–2 to the San Diego Mariners in the first round.

1975–76 Scores 26 goals and 29 assists for 55 points in 65 regular-season games with the Toros. Toronto finishes with the worst point total among the 12 teams that complete the season, and fails to make the playoffs.

1976–77 The Toronto Toros relocate to Birmingham, Alabama, over the off-season and become the Bulls. Paul scores 23 goals and 25 assists for 48 points in 81 regular-season games. The Bulls miss the playoffs.

1977–78 Scores 37 goals and 29 assists for 66 points in 80 regular-season games played with the Bulls. The Bulls finish sixth in the eight-team WHA, and meet Winnipeg in the first round of playoffs. Henderson scores a goal and adds an assist in the series, won 4–1 by the Jets.

1978–79 One of only three players over age 30 on a team known as the "Baby Bulls." Scores 24 goals and 27 assists for 51 points in 76 regular-season games with the Bulls, who do not qualify for the playoffs.

1979–80 The Birmingham Bulls, who are not one of the four WHA teams admitted to the NHL, join the minor-pro Central Hockey League. Paul continues to play for them, registering 17 goals and 18 assists for 35 points in 47 regular-season games. Also returns to the NHL with the Atlanta Flames, scoring 7 goals and 6 assists for 13 points in 30 regular-season games. Scores 2 goals against Toronto in his return to Maple Leaf Gardens. The Flames are defeated 3–1 in the first round of the playoffs. Henderson appears in all four games.

1980–81 Appears in 35 regular-season games with Birmingham, scoring 6 goals and 11 assists. Team disbands before the season is over. Rather than join the parent Calgary Flames, Henderson chooses to retire.

1984 Begins helping men develop for leadership with the LeaderImpact Group, where he still works

today, and holds two Honorary Doctor of
Divinity degrees.

1995 Inducted into Canada's Sports Hall of Fame.

1997 In January, the Canadian Mint launches a
commemorative coin depicting Paul's goal in game
eight of the 1972 Summit Series. This is the first
time a living person other than the king or queen
has been depicted on a Canadian coin. Canada
Post introduces a stamp celebrating the moment.

1998 Receives the Ontario Special Achievement Award
for his contribution to minor hockey.

2002 Is awarded the Queen's Jubilee Award for
distinguished community service.

2011 In September, Henderson, along with his jersey
worn in the Summit Series, embarks on a tour of
eastern Canada, beginning in his hometown of
Lucknow, Ontario. By mid-February 2012, it has
stopped in more than 40 towns. In Montreal, he
is joined by Soviet goaltender Vladislav Tretiak
and Montreal Canadiens legend Yvan Cournoyer.
The trio participated in a ceremonial puck drop
at the Bell Centre on January 7, 2012.

2012 Celebrates the fortieth anniversary of the 1972
Canada–Russia Summit Series with his teammates in a month of festivities.

Paul for the Hall

PAUL HENDERSON HAS NOT BEEN INDUCTED INTO THE Hockey Hall of Fame and his thoughts on that are documented in this book. He has no problem with his not being in the Hall, but many Canadians don't feel the same way.

A new website has been created to garner support for his induction. It's at PutPaulIntheHall.com. The Hockey Hall of Fame does acknowledge his great career in a biography on its website, LegendsofHockey.net.

You can also get more information on the campaign to get Paul Henderson inducted into the Hockey Hall of Fame at HeritageHockey.com.

Cops for Cancer

PAUL HENDERSON'S SERIES-WINNING GOAL DURING the 1972 Summit Series was voted the Goal of the Century by the Canadian Press in the year 2000. Today, the new goal of the century is the eradication of cancer and the enhancement of the quality of life of people living with cancer.

As is documented in this book, Paul was himself diagnosed with lymphoma, a form of cancer that he continues to battle today. Since his diagnosis, Paul has worked tirelessly to help end cancer in our lifetimes.

Cops for Cancer, the Canadian Cancer Society, Fruit of the Loom, Heritage Hockey, and Paul have all partnered to create a program to help raise funds to support the continuing battle to eradicate cancer. A beautiful commemorative T-shirt is on sale throughout the country, with a portion of the proceeds going to assist in this fight.

Paul Henderson's "Goal of the Century" is now being used in the fight toward the modern Goal of the Century. The T-shirt features the famous picture of Paul celebrating The Goal moments after it went in, with Paul's signature underneath and the words "THE GOAL" running down the right side.

You can join in the fight to cure cancer by purchasing a shirt at HeritageHockey.com.

1972 Team Canada

TEAM CANADA REALLY WAS A TEAM. HERE ARE SOME profiles of the players and coaches, providing a bit of background on their accomplishments before and after the series.

DON AWREY
Born: July 18, 1943, Kitchener, Ontario

- Nicknamed "Elbows."
- Suffered from a congenital back condition that nearly cost him the ability to walk, let alone play hockey. Took the chance at an operation with a 50 percent success rate that he would walk again, and the surgery was a success.
- Played in two games in the 1972 Summit Series.
- Was a key player on three Stanley Cup–winning teams with Boston (1970, 1972) and Montreal (1976), but his name was not engraved on the Stanley Cup for his win with the Canadiens due to the fact that he did not dress in the playoffs. That rule was changed just a couple of years later. His name is still not on the Cup from that winning season.
- Played in 979 NHL games between 1963–64 and 1978–79 (31 goals, 158 assists, 189 points).
- Played in the 1974 All-Star Game.
- Started his own charter bus company after his playing career

was finished, in which he transported Boston Bruins fans from Boston to Montreal to watch games at the Montreal Forum.

- Is currently residing in Florida.

GORDON "RED" BERENSON
Born: December 8, 1939, Regina, Saskatchewan

- Played in two games in the 1972 Summit Series (one assist).
- Nicknamed "The Red Baron."
- Was a member of world-champion Belleville McFarlands, 1959.
- Became a star with the St. Louis Blues in 1968–69 (eighth in NHL in scoring with 35 goals and 47 assists for 82 points in 76 regular-season games; 7 goals, 3 assists, 10 points in 12 playoff games).
- Is the only player in NHL history to score 6 goals in 1 game on the road (November 7, 1968, at Philadelphia).
- Played in 987 NHL games between 1961–62 and 1977–78 (261 goals, 397 assists, 658 points).
- Played in five All-Star games (1965, 1969–72, 1974).
- Won Jack Adams Award as NHL Coach of the Year, 1980–81.
- Has been head coach of the University of Michigan Wolverines since 1984, winning NCAA championships in 1996 and 1998.

GARY BERGMAN
Born: October 7, 1938, Kenora, Ontario
Died: December 8, 2000 (age 62)

- Won the Turnbull Cup (Manitoba Junior Hockey League Champions) as a member of the Winnipeg Braves in 1959. The Braves also went on that year to win the Memorial Cup by defeating the Peterborough TPT Petes (4–1).
- Played in all eight games of the 1972 Summit Series, registering three assists.

- Played 838 NHL games between 1964–65 and 1975–76 (68 goals, 299 assists, 367 points) for the Detroit Red Wings, Minnesota North Stars, and Kansas City Scouts.
- Played in the 1973 All-Star Game.
- Captained the Detroit Red Wings in the 1973–74 season.
- Is an honoured member of both Canada's Sport Hall of Fame and the Manitoba Hockey Hall of Fame.

WAYNE CASHMAN
Born: June 24, 1945, Kingston, Ontario

- Nicknamed "Cash."
- Played in two games in the 1972 Summit Series, assisting on two goals and compiling 14 penalty minutes.
- Played in 1,027 NHL games between 1964–65 and 1982–83, all with the Boston Bruins (277 goals, 516 assists, 793 points).
- Played left wing on a line with Phil Esposito and Ken Hodge, forming one of the most dangerous forward units in the NHL.
- Was a member of two Stanley Cup champions (1970, 1972).
- Was Second Team All-Star at left wing, 1974.
- Played in the 1974 All-Star Game.
- Was seventh in the NHL in scoring in 1970–71 (21 goals, 58 assists, 79 points) and fourth in 1973–74 (30 goals, 59 assists, 89 points).
- Captained the Bruins from 1978–1983.
- Was the last player from the "Original Six" era to retire.
- Was head coach of Philadelphia Flyers for 61 games in 1997–98 (32–20–9).
- Was assistant coach of New York Rangers, Tampa Bay Lightning, San Jose Sharks, Philadelphia Flyers, and Boston Bruins between 1987 and 2006.

- Was a member of the Team Canada coaching staff for the 1998 Nagano Olympics.

BOBBY CLARKE
Born: August 13, 1949, Flin Flon, Manitoba

- Played in all eight games in the 1972 Summit Series, scoring two goals and four assists for six points, while collecting 18 minutes in penalties.
- Played in 1,144 NHL games between 1969–70 and 1983–84, all with Philadelphia (358 goals, 852 assists, 1,210 points).
- Won the Hart Trophy as the NHL's most valuable player three times (1973, 1975, 1976).
- Won the Frank Selke Trophy as the NHL's top defensive forward in 1983.
- Won the Bill Masterton Trophy (for perseverance and sportsmanship) in 1972.
- Won the Lester B. Pearson Award (as the NHL Players' Association's choice as most valuable player), 1972–73.
- Was Second Team All-Star at centre, 1972–73 and 1973–74.
- Was First Team All-Star at centre, 1974–75 and 1975–76.
- Was captain of Stanley Cup championship teams, 1974 and 1975.
- Was captain of Team Canada at 1976 Canada Cup.
- Played in eight All-Star games (1970–75, 1977–78).
- Led NHL in assists, 1974–75 (89) and 1975–76 (89).
- Topped 100 points three times (1972–73, 1974–75, 1975–76).
- Became an officer of the Order of Canada, 1981.
- Earned a bronze medal at the 1982 World Championships in Finland.
- Was general manager of the Philadelphia Flyers (1984–1990, 1994–2006), Minnesota North Stars (1990–92), and Florida

Panthers (1993–94); teams reached Stanley Cup Finals in 1985, 1987, 1991, and 1997.

- Was inducted into the Hockey Hall of Fame in 1987.
- Was general manager of Team Canada at 1998 Winter Olympics in Nagano, Japan.
- Is currently the senior vice president of the Philadelphia Flyers, since December 2006.

YVAN COURNOYER
Born: November 22, 1943, Drummondville, Quebec

- Played in all eight games in the 1972 Summit Series, scoring three goals and two assists for five points.
- Was known as "The Roadrunner," for his blinding speed.
- Played in 968 NHL games between 1963–64 and 1978–79, all with Montreal (428 goals, 435 assists, 863 points).
- Was captain of Montreal Canadiens, 1975–78.
- Was a member of 10 Stanley Cup championship teams (1965, 1966, 1968, 1969, 1971, 1973, 1976–79).
- Played in six All-Star games (1967, 1971–74, 1978).
- Won Conn Smythe Trophy as playoff MVP in 1973.
- Scored Stanley Cup–clinching goal in 1973.
- Was second Team All-Star at right wing in 1969, 1971, 1972, and 1973.
- Was sixth in NHL in scoring in 1968–69 (43 goals, 44 assists, 87 points) and eighth in 1971–72 (47 goals, 36 assists, 83 points).
- Led NHL in power-play goals, 1966–67 (20).
- Led NHL in game-winning goals in 1975–76 (12), and tied for lead in 1966–67 (7).
- Retired after the 1978–1979 season due to back problems.
- Was inducted into the Hockey Hall of Fame in 1982.
- Coached the Montreal Roadrunners during the 1994–95 season.

- Was assistant coach of the Montreal Canadiens during the 1996–97 season.
- Currently serves as an official ambassador for the Montreal Canadiens.

MARCEL DIONNE
Born: August 3, 1951, Drummondville, Quebec

- Although selected for Team Canada, did not play in the 1972 Summit Series.
- Nicknamed "The Little Beaver."
- Was selected second overall by Detroit in the 1971 Amateur Draft.
- Played in 1,348 NHL games between 1971–72 and 1988–89 (731 goals, 1,040 assists, 1,771 points) for the Detroit Red Wings, Los Angeles Kings, and New York Rangers.
- Played in eight All-Star games (1975–78, 1980, 1981, 1983, 1985).
- Won the Lady Byng Trophy as NHL's most gentlemanly player twice (1974–75, 1976–77).
- Won the Lester B. Pearson Trophy as NHL Players' Association's choice as MVP twice (1978–79, 1979–80).
- Won the Art Ross Trophy as NHL's leading scorer in 1979–80.
- Was first Team All-Star at centre, 1976–77 and 1979–80.
- Was second Team All-Star at centre, 1978–79 and 1980–81.
- Scored at least 50 goals six times (1976–77, 1978–79 through 1982–83) and at least 100 points eight times (1974–75, 1976–77, 1978–79 through 1982–83, 1984–85).
- Played for Team Canada in 1976 and 1981 Canada Cups as well as six World Championships (1977–79, 1982, 1983, 1986).
- Is fifth on the NHL's all-time point-scoring list, behind Wayne Gretzky, Mark Messier, Gordie Howe, and Ron Francis.

- Is fourth on the NHL's all-time goal-scoring list, behind Gretzky, Howe, and Brett Hull.
- Was inducted into the Hockey Hall of Fame in 1992.
- In January 2004, Canada Post featured Dionne and five other NHL All-Stars on a postage stamp as part of the NHL All-Stars Collection.
- The Centre Civique Arena in Drummondville, Quebec, was renamed Centre Marcel Dionne after he retired.
- Currently resides in Niagara Falls, Ontario, where he runs and operates Marcel Dionne Incorporated, a vast sports memorabilia store. He is also a royal ambassador for the Los Angeles Kings.

KEN DRYDEN
Born: August 8, 1947, Hamilton, Ontario

- Played four games in the 1972 Summit Series (2–2, 4.75 goals-against average).
- Was the goaltender for the crucial game eight, which Canada won to clinch the series.
- Was selected fourteenth overall by Boston in the 1964 Amateur Draft.
- Joined the Montreal Canadiens with six games to go in the 1970–71 season.
- Won the Stanley Cup with the Canadiens that season, while capturing the Conn Smythe Trophy as playoff MVP.
- Won the Calder Trophy as rookie of the year the following season.
- Was a member of six Stanley Cup champions (1971, 1973, 1976–79).
- Played in five All-Star games (1972, 1975–78).
- Won the Vezina Trophy five times (1972–73, 1975–76 through 1978–79).

- Was second Team All-Star in goal, 1971–72.
- Was first Team All-Star in goal five times (1972–73, 1975–76 through 1978–79).
- Led NHL in wins, 1971–72, 1972–73, 1975–76, and 1976–77.
- Led NHL in goals-against average, 1972–73, 1975–76, 1977–78, and 1978–79.
- Played in 397 NHL games; career record 258–57–74 with a 2.24 goals-against average and 46 shutouts.
- Ken's career winning percentage of .758 is the best in NHL history among goaltenders.
- Was a colour commentator for the Miracle on Ice during the 1980 Lake Placid Olympics.
- Was inducted into the Hockey Hall of Fame in 1983.
- Wrote his second book, his first post-retirement from the NHL, titled *The Game*, in 1983. Was nominated for a Governor General's Award. He has written six books in total.
- Became president of the Toronto Maple Leafs in 1997.
- Resigned from the hockey world in 2004 when he began his pursuit of politics.
- Joined the Liberal Party of Canada and ran for federal election in June 2004. He was re-elected in 2006, but lost his cabinet seat in the 2011 federal election.

RON ELLIS
Born: January 8, 1945, Lindsay, Ontario

- Played in all eight games of the Summit Series on a line with Bobby Clarke and Paul Henderson, registering three assists.
- Played in 1,034 NHL games, all with the Toronto Maple Leafs (332 goals, 308 assists, 640 points).
- Tied for lead in NHL in game-winning goals in 1966–67 (7).
- Was a member of the last Toronto Maple Leaf team to win

the Stanley Cup in 1967.

- Played in four All-Star games (1964, 1965, 1968, 1970).
- Played for Team Canada in 1977 World Championships.
- Became the director of public affairs for the Hockey Hall of Fame in 1992.
- Founded The Ron Ellis Team Canada Foundation.
- Co-wrote his biography *Over the Boards: The Ron Ellis Story*.
- Works closely with the Centre for Addiction and Mental Health, spreading awareness of the stigma associated with depression.

PHIL ESPOSITO
Born: February 20, 1942, Sault Ste. Marie, Ontario

- Was assistant captain of Team Canada 1972. Led the team in scoring with 7 goals and 6 assists for 13 points in the 8-game series.
- Played in 1,282 NHL games between 1963–64 and 1980–81 (717 goals, 873 assists, 1,590 points) for the Chicago Blackhawks, Boston Bruins, and New York Rangers.
- Began his career with the Chicago Blackhawks; traded to Boston in 1967.
- Was a member of two Stanley Cup–winning teams with the Bruins (1970, 1972).
- Was the first player in NHL history to reach 100 points, in 1968–69; finished the season with 126 points.
- Set NHL records with 76 goals and 152 points in 76 games, 1970–71.
- Played in 10 All-Star games (1969–75, 1977, 1978, 1980).
- Won Art Ross Trophy as the NHL's leading scorer five times (1968–69, 1970–71, 1971–72, 1972–73, 1973–74).
- Won Hart Trophy as the NHL's most valuable player twice (1968–69 and 1973–74).

- Won the Lester B. Pearson Trophy as the NHLPA's choice as most valuable player twice (1970–71, 1973–74).
- Won the Lou Marsh Trophy as Canada's male athlete of the year, 1972.
- Was First Team All-Star at centre six times (1968–69 through 1973–74).
- Was Second Team All-Star at centre twice (1967–68, 1974–75).
- Led NHL in goals six consecutive seasons, 1969–70 through 1974–75.
- Led NHL in assists three times (1967–68, 1968–69, 1972–73).
- Is fifth on the NHL's all-time goal-scoring list, behind Wayne Gretzky, Gordie Howe, Brett Hull, and Marcel Dionne.
- Captained the New York Rangers from 1975–78.
- Also played for Team Canada at 1976 Canada Cup and 1977 World Championships.
- Was head coach of New York Rangers in 1986–87 (43 games) and 1988–89 (2 games).
- Was general manager of New York Rangers (1986–89) and Tampa Bay Lightning (1991–98).
- Co-founded the Tampa Bay Lightning.
- Has also been a Ranger and Lightning broadcaster.
- Was made an officer of the Order of Canada, 1972.
- Was inducted into the Hockey Hall of Fame in 1984.
- Is currently the colour commentator for Tampa Bay Lightning radio broadcasts.

TONY ESPOSITO
Born: April 23, 1943, Sault Ste. Marie, Ontario

- Played in four games in the 1972 Summit Series and went 2–1–1 with a 3.25 goals-against average.
- Won the all-important game two at Maple Leaf Gardens and

the crucial game seven in Moscow.

- Won an NCAA championship with Michigan Tech, 1964–65.
- Won the Calder Trophy as rookie of the year in 1969–70. Won the Vezina Trophy the same season and was runner-up for the Hart Trophy. His 15 shutouts were the most by an NHL goaltender since 1928–29.
- Also won the Vezina Trophy in 1971–72 and 1973–74.
- Led NHL in wins, 1969–70 and 1970–71.
- Led NHL in goals-against average in 1971–72 (1.77).
- Led NHL in shutouts three times (1969–70, 1971–72, 1979–80).
- Played in six All-Star games (1970–74, 1980).
- Was First Team All-Star in goal (1969–70, 1971–72, 1979–80).
- Second Team All-Star in goal (1972–73, 1973–74).
- Played in 886 NHL games, with a record of 423–306–151, a 2.92 goals-against average, and 76 shutouts.
- Was third all-time in wins by a goaltender when he retired, trailing only Terry Sawchuk and Jacques Plante (is currently seventh).
- Also played for Team Canada at the 1977 World Championships, but played for Team USA at the 1981 Canada Cup.
- Retired from his NHL playing career in 1985, became general manager of the Pittsburgh Penguins in 1988–89.
- Was inducted into Hockey Hall of Fame, 1988.
- Was chief scout for the Tampa Bay Lighting from 1991–98.
- Became an official ambassador of the Chicago Blackhawks in March 2008.

JOHN FERGUSON
Born: September 5, 1938, Vancouver, British Columbia
Died: July 14, 2007 (age 68)

- Was invited to play for Team Canada 1972 (he had retired from the NHL after the 1970–71 season), but he declined, instead accepting the position of assistant coach.
- Played in 500 NHL games between 1963–64 and 1970–71, all with the Montreal Canadiens (145 goals, 158 assists, 303 points, 1,214 penalty minutes).
- Played for five Stanley Cup champions (1964–65, 1965–66, 1967–68, 1968–69, 1970–71).
- Was a rare blend of toughness and skill; scored at least 20 goals twice, while leading the league in penalty minutes with 177 in 1966–67.
- Montreal linemates included Jean Beliveau and Claude Provost.
- Played in two All-Star games (1965, 1967); MVP of the 1967 game.
- Scored Stanley Cup–clinching goal in 1969.
- Was head coach of New York Rangers, 1976–77, and Winnipeg Jets, 1986.
- Was general manager of the Rangers, 1976–78, and Winnipeg Jets, 1978–88.
- Worked for the Ottawa Senators in the early 1990s.
- Was a special consultant to the general manager of the San Jose Sharks.

ROD GILBERT
Born: July 1, 1941, Montreal, Quebec

- Played six games in the 1972 Summit Series, scoring four points and collecting nine penalty minutes.
- Played in 1,065 NHL games between 1960–61 and 1977–78, all with New York Rangers (406 goals, 615 assists, 1,021 points).
- Played on the famous GAG (Goal-a-Game) Line with Vic Hadfield and Jean Ratelle.
- Set 20 team scoring records including career goals (406), career points (1021) and assists in one game (5, which he did 3 times).
- Played in eight All-Star games (1964, 1965, 1967, 1969, 1970, 1972, 1975, 1977).
- Won the Bill Masterton Trophy for perseverance and sportsmanship, 1975–76.
- Was Second Team All-Star at right wing, 1967–68.
- Was First Team All-Star at right wing, 1971–72.
- Also played for Team Canada at 1977 World Championships.
- Became the first Ranger to have his number (7) retired by the club.
- Was Head coach of New Haven Nighthawks (AHL), 1980–81.
- Won the Lester Patrick Trophy for contributions to hockey in the United States, 1991.
- Was inducted into the Hockey Hall of Fame in 1982.
- Opened his own restaurant called "Gilbert's" in Manhattan.
- Was awarded the Ellis Island Medal of Honour in recognition of his humanitarian efforts.
- Currently works as director of special projects and community relations representative for the New York Rangers.

BRIAN GLENNIE
Born: August 29, 1946, Toronto, Ontario

- Did not appear in the 1972 Summit Series.
- Was captain of the Memorial Cup champion Toronto Marlboros, 1966–67.
- Played for the Canadian National Team in 1967–68 and represented Canada at the 1968 Winter Olympics in Grenoble, France, winning a bronze medal.
- Played in 572 NHL games between 1969–70 and 1978–79 (14 goals, 100 assists, 114 points), primarily with the Toronto Maple Leafs.
- Was a solid defenceman known for his devastating bodychecks.
- Was inducted into Canada's Sports Hall of Fame, 2005.

BILL GOLDSWORTHY
Born: August 24, 1944, Kitchener, Ontario
Died: March 29, 1996 (age 51)

- Played in three games in the 1972 Summit Series, scoring two points.
- Originally with the Boston Bruins, Bill became a star and fan favourite with the Minnesota North Stars beginning with the 1967–68 season.
- Played in 771 NHL games (283 goals, 258 assists, 541 points) with Boston, Minnesota, and the New York Rangers between 1964–65 and 1977–78.
- Played in 49 WHA games (12 goals, 12 assists, 24 points) with Indianapolis and Edmonton, 1977–78 and 1978–79.
- Played in four All-Star games (1970, 1972, 1974, 1976).
- Scored a career-high 48 goals in 1973–74.
- Coached the Indianapolis Racers (WHA), for 29 games in 1977–78 and the San Antonio Iguanas (CHL) in 1994–95.

JOCELYN GUEVREMONT
Born: March 1, 1951, Ste. Rose, Quebec

- Did not appear in the 1972 Summit Series.
- Was selected to the team after playing only 75 NHL games.
- Was selected third overall by the Vancouver Canucks in the 1971 Amateur Draft.
- Was a member of Memorial Cup–champion Montreal Junior Canadiens, 1969 and 1970.
- Played in 571 NHL games with Vancouver, Buffalo, and New York Rangers (84 goals, 223 assists, 307 points) between 1971–72 and 1979–80.
- Played in the 1974 All-Star Game.
- Retired from the NHL in 1980 due to chronic shoulder problems.

VIC HADFIELD
Born: October 4, 1940, Oakville, Ontario

- Played in two games of the 1972 Summit Series.
- Was captain of the New York Rangers, 1971–74.
- Was the first 50-goal scorer in New York Rangers history.
- Played on the Famous GAG (Goal-a-Game) Line with Rod Gilbert and Jean Ratelle.
- Played in 1,002 NHL games between 1961–62 and 1976–77 (323 goals, 389 assists, 712 points).
- Played in two All-Star games (1965, 1972).
- Owns the Vic Hadfield Golf & Learning Centre in Oakville, Ontario.

PAUL HENDERSON
Born: January 28, 1943, Kincardine, Ontario

- Scored 7 goals and 3 assists for 10 points in the 1972 Summit Series.
- Scored the winning goals in games six, seven, and eight.
- His goal in the eighth game with 34 seconds remaining is regarded as The Goal of The Century.
- The goal gave Canada the victory in the series over the Soviets.
- Made NHL debut in 1963 with the Detroit Red Wings.
- Was traded to the Toronto Maple Leafs in 1968 in a transaction that included two future Hall of Famers – Frank Mahovlich and Norm Ullman.
- Played in 707 NHL games (236 goals, 241 assists, 477 points).
- Played in 360 WHA games (140 goals, 143 assists, 283 points) with Toronto/Birmingham.
- Played in two All-Star games (1972, 1973).

DENNIS HULL
Born: November 19, 1944, Pointe-Anne, Ontario

- Played in four games in the Summit Series, scoring four points, including two goals.
- Played in 959 NHL games – 904 with Chicago, 55 with Detroit (303 goals, 351 assists, 654 points).
- Played in five All-Star games (1969, 1971–74).
- Was Second Team All-Star at left wing, 1972–73.
- Graduated from Brock University with a degree in history and physical education, taught at Ridley College, and became a broadcaster, all following his NHL career.
- Was athletic director at Illinois Institute of Technology after retirement.
- Wrote a book titled *The Third Best Hull*.

- Is a popular and entertaining public speaker/comedian. Among his many appearances has been the Winnipeg Comedy Festival, which he hosted.
- Operates a cattle farm in Northumberland County, Ontario, with his brother Gary.

ED JOHNSTON
Born: November 23, 1935, Montreal, Quebec

- Did not appear in 1972 Summit Series.
- Won two Stanley Cups with the Boston Bruins (1970, 1972).
- Was the last goaltender to play in every minute of every game for his team during a season, the Boston Bruins of 1962–63.
- Played in 592 NHL games with Boston, Toronto, St. Louis, and Chicago between 1962–63 and 1977–78, with a record of 234–257–80, a 3.25 goals-against average, and 32 shutouts.
- Coached Chicago Blackhawks (1979–80) and Pittsburgh Penguins (1980–83, 1993–97).
- Was general manager in Pittsburgh (1983–88) and Hartford (1989–92). Worked in Penguins front office, 1997–2009.

GUY LAPOINTE
Born: March 18, 1948, Montreal, Quebec

- Played in seven games of the 1972 Summit Series, recording one assist.
- Nicknamed "Pointu."
- Played in 884 NHL games between 1968–69 and 1983–84 (171 goals, 451 assists, 622 points) for the Montreal Canadiens, St. Louis Blues, and Boston Bruins.
- Played on six Stanley Cup champions with Montreal (1971, 1973, 1976–79).
- Played in four All-Star Games (1973, 1975–77).

- Was First Team All-Star on defence, 1972–73.
- Was Second Team All-Star on defence, 1974–75 through 1976–77.
- Was part of Montreal's Big Three on defence that included Serge Savard and Larry Robinson, both of whom are also Hall of Fame defencemen.
- Also played for Team Canada in 1976 Canada Cup.
- Was inducted into the Hockey Hall of Fame in 1993.
- Has worked for the Minnesota Wild as coordinator of amateur scouting since 1999.

FRANK MAHOVLICH
Born: January 10, 1938, Timmins, Ontario

- Played six games in the Summit Series, collecting two points.
- Nicknamed "The Big M."
- Won Calder Trophy as rookie of the year, 1957–58, edging out Bobby Hull.
- Played in 1,181 NHL games between 1956–57 and 1973–74 (533 goals, 570 assists, 1,103 points) with Toronto, Detroit, and Montreal.
- Played in 237 WHA games between 1974–75 and 1977–78 (89 goals, 143 assists, 232 points), all with Toronto/ Birmingham.
- Won four Stanley Cups with Toronto Maple Leafs (1962–64, 1967) and two more with Montreal (1971, 1973).
- Played in 15 All-Star games (1959–65, 1967–74).
- Was First Team All-Star at left wing (1960–61, 1962–63, 1972–73).
- Was Second Team All-Star at left wing (1961–62, 1963–64 through 1965–66, 1968–69, 1969–70).
- Also played for Team Canada in 1974 Summit Series.
- Was inducted into the Hockey Hall of Fame in 1981.

- Became a member of the Order of Canada, 1994.
- Appointed to the Canadian Senate, 1998.

PETER MAHOVLICH
Born: October 10, 1946, Timmins, Ontario

- Played in seven games in the 1972 Summit Series, scoring a goal and adding an assist.
- The goal was scored in game two at Maple Leaf Gardens. The goal was scored shorthanded and secured the victory for Team Canada.
- Nicknamed "The Little M."
- Was drafted second overall by Detroit in the 1963 Amateur Draft.
- Played in 884 NHL games with Detroit, Montreal, and Pittsburgh between 1965–66 and 1980–81 (288 goals, 485 assists, 773 points).
- Played in two All-Star games (1971, 1976).
- Was a member of four Stanley Cup–winning teams with Montreal (1971, 1973, 1976, 1977).
- Coached several minor-pro teams including the Toledo Goaldiggers, Colorado Rangers, Denver Rangers, Forth Worth Fire, and Cape Breton Oilers.
- Scouted for the Edmonton Oilers from 1995–97, then for the Tampa Bay Lightning.
- Is currently a pro scout with the Florida Panthers.

RICHARD MARTIN
Born: July 26, 1951, Verdun, Quebec
Died: March 13, 2011 (aged 59)

- Did not appear in the 1972 Summit Series.
- Was selected fifth overall by Buffalo in the 1971 Amateur Draft.

- Was named to Team Canada 1972 after appearing in only 73 NHL games.
- Set a rookie goal-scoring record (since broken) with 44 in 1971–72.
- Combined with Gilbert Perreault and Rene Robert to form the feared French Connection for the Buffalo Sabres.
- Played in 685 NHL games between 1971–72 and 1981–82 (384 goals, 317 assists, 701 points) for the Sabres, including four games with the Los Angeles Kings.
- Suffered knee injury in November 1980 that effectively ended his career.
- Had back-to-back 52-goal seasons, 1973–74 and 1974–75.
- Played in seven All-Star games (1972–78).
- Was First Team All-Star at left wing, 1973–74 and 1974–75.
- Was Second Team All-Star at left wing, 1975–76 and 1976–77.
- Was inducted into the Greater Buffalo Sports Hall of Fame in 2005.

STAN MIKITA
Born: May 20, 1940, Sokolce, Czechoslovakia

- Played two games in the Summit Series and recorded one assist.
- In 1966–67, became the first player to win three trophies in one season: Hart (MVP), Art Ross (scoring champion), and Lady Byng (most gentlemanly player).
- Won all three trophies again in 1967–68.
- Also won Art Ross Trophy in 1963–64 and 1964–65.
- Won a Stanley Cup with the Blackhawks in 1960–61.
- Became one of the first players to experiment with a curved blade for his stick.

- Played in 1,394 NHL games between 1958–59 and 1979–80 (541 goals, 926 assists, 1,467 points), all with Chicago.
- Played in nine All-Star games (1964, 1967–69, 1971–75).
- Led NHL in assists, 1964–65 through 1966–67.
- Won the Lester Patrick Trophy for contributions to hockey in the United States, 1976.
- Had the NHL's third-highest career point total, trailing only Gordie Howe and Phil Esposito (is currently fourteenth).
- Was inducted into the Hockey Hall of Fame in 1983.
- Was inducted into the Slovak Hockey Hall of Fame in 2002.
- Currently serves as an ambassador of goodwill for the Chicago Blackhawks.
- A statue of Mikita and former teammate Bobby Hull were unveiled outside the United Centre, the home of the Blackhawks, in 2011.

JEAN-PAUL PARISE
Born: December 11, 1941, Smooth Rock Falls, Ontario

- Played six games in the Summit Series, scoring four points and compiling an impressive 28 minutes in penalties, most of which came in the first period of game eight.
- Nicknamed "Jeep."
- Played in 890 NHL games between 1965–66 and 1978–79, primarily with the Minnesota North Stars and New York Islanders (238 goals, 356 assists, 594 points), which also included time with the Boston Bruins, Toronto Maple Leafs, and Cleveland Barons.
- Played in two All-Star games (1970, 1973).
- Was a solid two-way left-winger who set career highs in goals (27) and points (75) in 1972–73.
- Was an assistant coach with Minnesota between 1980–88

(with the exception of 1984, when he was the head coach of the North Star's minor league affiliate Salt Lake Golden Eagles of the Central Hockey League).

- Became a coach and director of hockey at the Shattuck-Saint Mary's School (alumni include Sidney Crosby, Jonathan Toews, Jack Johnson, and Parise's son Zach).
- Was named head coach and general manager of the Des Moines Buccaneers of the United States Hockey League for the 2008–09 season, and an assistant the following year.

BRAD PARK
Born: July 6, 1948, Toronto, Ontario

- Played in all eight games of the Summit Series, compiling a goal and four assists.
- Was selected second overall by New York Rangers in the 1966 Amateur Draft.
- Played in 1,113 NHL games between 1968–69 and 1984–85 (213 goals, 683 assists, 896 points) for the New York Rangers, Boston Bruins, and Detroit Red Wings.
- Played in nine All-Star games (1970–78).
- First Team All-Star on defence (1969–70, 1971–72, 1973–74, 1975–76, 1977–78).
- Second Team All-Star on defence (1970–71, 1972–73).
- Was involved in blockbuster trade between New York and Boston in 1975 that sent Park and Jean Ratelle to the Bruins for Phil Esposito and Carol Vadnais.
- Won the Bill Masterton Trophy for perseverance and sportsmanship, 1983–84.
- Following his retirement in 1985, he served briefly as the Red Wings head coach in 1986.
- Was inducted into the Hockey Hall of Fame, 1988.

GILBERT PERREAULT
Born: November 13, 1950, Victoriaville, Quebec

- Played two games in the Summit Series, scoring two points.
- Was selected first overall by Buffalo in the 1970 Amateur Draft.
- Combined with Richard Martin and Rene Robert to form the feared French Connection line with the Buffalo Sabres during the 1970s.
- Played in 1,191 NHL games, all with Buffalo (512 goals, 814 assists, 1,326 points).
- Topped 100 points twice (113 in 1975–76 and 106 in 1979–80).
- Played in six All-Star games (1971, 1972, 1977, 1978, 1980, 1984).
- Won the Calder Trophy as rookie of the year, 1970–71.
- Won the Lady Byng Trophy as the NHL's most gentlemanly player, 1972–73.
- Was second Team All-Star at centre, 1975–76 and 1976–77.
- Also represented Canada in 1976 and 1981 Canada Cups.
- Won two Memorial Cup championships with Montreal Junior Canadiens, 1969 and 1970.
- Was the only player in Buffalo Sabres history to record a seven-point game.
- Was inducted into the Buffalo Sabres Hall of Fame in 1989.
- Was inducted into the Hockey Hall of Fame, 1990.
- Following his retirement, coached in the Quebec Major Junior Hockey League, as well as invested in real estate.
- Is currently the corporate and community relations liaison for the Buffalo Sabres.

JEAN RATELLE
Born: October 3, 1940, Lac St. Jean, Quebec

- Played six games in the Summit Series, scoring a goal and adding three assists.
- Played with Vic Hadfield and Rod Gilbert on the New York Rangers' GAG (Goal-a-Game) Line.
- Played in 1,281 NHL games between 1960–61 and 1980–81 (491 goals, 776 assists, 1,267 points) with the New York Rangers and Boston Bruins.
- Topped 100 points in 1971–72 (109) and 1975–76 (105).
- Played in five All-Star games (1970–73, 1980).
- Won the Lady Byng Trophy (most gentlemanly player), 1971–72, 1975–76.
- Won the Lester B. Pearson Award as NHLPA's choice as MVP, 1971–72.
- Won the Bill Masterton Trophy for perseverance and sportsmanship, 1970–71.
- Was Second Team All-Star at centre, 1971–72.
- Was involved in blockbuster trade between New York and Boston in 1975 that sent Ratelle and Brad Park to the Bruins for Phil Esposito and Carol Vadnais.
- Retired as a member of the Boston Bruins in 1981.
- Was assistant coach of the Bruins from 1981–85.
- Was inducted into the Hockey Hall of Fame, 1985.

MICKEY REDMOND
Born: December 27, 1947, Kirkland Lake, Ontario

- Played in one game in the 1972 Summit Series (no points).
- Was the first player in Detroit Red Wing history to score 50 goals.
- Was a member of two Stanley Cup–winning teams with the Montreal Canadiens (1968, 1969).

- Played in 538 NHL games between 1967–68 and 1975–76 (233 goals, 195 assists, 428 points) with the Canadiens and Detroit Red Wings before a back injury forced him to retire.
- Scored 52 goals in 1972–73, 51 in 1973–74.
- Played in the 1974 All-Star Game.
- Was First Team All-Star at right wing, 1972–73.
- Was Second Team All-Star at right wing, 1973–74.
- Since retirement, has had a long-running career as a broadcaster, which currently involves colour commentary for the Detroit Red Wings. He also had a stint on *Hockey Night in Canada*.

SERGE SAVARD
Born: January 22, 1946, Montreal, Quebec

- Played in five games in the Summit Series, compiling two assists.
- Played in all four of Team Canada's wins.
- Nicknamed "The Senator."
- A hairline fracture limited his playing time in the Summit Series.
- Won eight Stanley Cups with the Montreal Canadiens (1968, 1969, 1971, 1973, 1976–79).
- Played in 1,040 NHL games between 1966–67 and 1982–83 (106 goals, 333 assists, 439 points) with the Canadiens and the Winnipeg Jets.
- Set career highs with 20 goals and 60 points in 1974–75.
- Was the first defenceman to capture the Conn Smythe Trophy, 1968–69.
- Won the Bill Masterton Trophy for perseverance and sportsmanship, 1978–79.
- Was Second Team All-Star on defence, 1978–79.
- Was part of Montreal's Big Three on defence that included Guy Lapointe and Larry Robinson, both of whom are also

Hall of Fame defencemen.

- Was general manager of the Montreal Canadiens, 1983–95, while also managing Montreal's junior affiliate the Sherbrooke Canadiens, where he helped guide the team to a Calder Cup in 1985.
- Won two more Stanley Cups as Canadiens' GM, 1986 and 1993.
- Became an officer of the Order of Canada, 1994.
- Was inducted into the Hockey Hall of Fame, 1986.
- Was made a knight of the National Order of Quebec in 2004.
- Became a partner in a firm of real estate developers.
- Was part-owner of the QMJHL's PEI Rocket with his son Serge Savard Jr.

ROD SEILING
Born: November 14, 1944, Elmira, Ontario

- Played in three games in the 1972 Summit Series.
- Also represented Canada at the Winter Olympics in Innsbruck, Austria, in 1964.
- Played in the 1972 All-Star Game.
- Played in 979 NHL games between 1962–63 and 1978–79 (62 goals, 269 assists, 331 points).
- Was involved in a seven-player trade between Toronto and New York in February 1964. Seiling, Dick Duff, Bob Nevin, and Arnie Brown went to the Rangers in exchange for Andy Bathgate and Don McKenney.
- Was a steady stay-at-home defenceman
- Since 2006, has been chair of the Ontario Racing Commission.
- Was also president and CEO of the Greater Toronto Hotel Association.

HARRY SINDEN
Born: September 14, 1932, Collins Bay, Ontario

- Was head coach of Team Canada 1972.
- Was a member of Allan Cup–winning Whitby Dunlops in 1957 and 1959.
- Represented Canada at the 1958 World Championships (Canada won the gold medal) and the 1960 Winter Olympics in Squaw Valley, California (silver medal).
- Was named top defenceman in Eastern Professional Hockey League, 1961–62 (shared award with Jean Gauthier) and 1962–63.
- Was most valuable player in Eastern Professional Hockey League, 1962–63.
- Was head coach of Boston Bruins, 1966–67 to 1969–70 (also brief stints in 1979–80 and 1984–85).
- Coached Bruins to Stanley Cup championship in 1970.
- Was general manager of the Bruins, 1972–2000.
- Was president of the Bruins, 1989–2006.
- Continues to serve as a senior adviser to the Bruins' ownership.
- Is a member of the selection committee of the Hockey Hall of Fame.
- Was inducted into the Hockey Hall of Fame as a builder, 1983.

PAT STAPLETON
Born: July 4, 1940, Sarnia, Ontario

- Played in seven games in the Summit Series (no points).
- Was a solid, stay-at-home defenceman paired with Bill White in the series to form a superb defensive duo.
- Played in 635 NHL games between 1961–62 and 1972–73 (43 goals, 294 assists, 337 points) with the Boston Bruins and Chicago Blackhawks.

- Played in 372 WHA games between 1973–74 and 1977–78 (27 goals, 212 assists, 238 points).
- Also played for, and was captain of, Team Canada in the 1974 Summit Series.
- Won Dennis Murphy Trophy (top defenceman in the WHA), 1973–74.
- Played in four All-Star games (1967, 1969, 1971, 1972).
- Was Second Team All-Star at defence (1965–66, 1970–71, 1971–72).
- Was WHA First Team All-Star at defence, 1973–74.
- Was WHA Second Team All-Star at defence, 1975–76.
- Was head coach of the WHA Chicago Cougars (1973–75) and Indianapolis Racers (1978–79).
- Is a member of the advisory board of the Junior B Strathroy Rockets of the Western Ontario Junior Hockey League.

DALE TALLON
Born: October 19, 1950, Noranda, Quebec

- Did not appear in the 1972 Summit Series.
- Was selected second overall by the Vancouver Canucks in the 1970 Amateur Draft.
- Played in two All-Star games (1971, 1972).
- Played in 642 NHL games between 1970–71 and 1979–80 (98 goals, 238 assists, 336 points) with the Vancouver Canucks, Chicago Blackhawks, and Pittsburgh Penguins.
- Set career high in goals (17) in 1971–72 and points (62) in 1975–76.
- Won the Canadian Junior Golf Championship in 1969. Has played on the Canadian PGA Tour.
- After his retirement in 1979–80, became a broadcaster for the Chicago Blackhawks.

- Was Blackhawks director of player personnel from 1998–2002.
- Was assistant general manager of the Chicago Blackhawks from 2003–05.
- Was general manager of the Chicago Blackhawks from 2005–09.
- Became senior advisor of the Blackhawks in July 2009.
- Became general manager of the Florida Panthers in May 2010.
- Although the Chicago Blackhawks won the Stanley Cup in June 2010 after Tallon's departure to Florida, his name was still engraved on the Cup for being such a large contributor to the development of the championship team.

BILL WHITE
Born: August 26, 1939, Toronto, Ontario

- Played seven games in the Summit Series, scoring a goal and adding an assist.
- Was paired with Pat Stapleton in the series to form a solid duo on defence.
- Was 28 when he made his NHL debut with Los Angeles in 1967.
- Played in 604 NHL games between 1967–68 and 1975–76 for the Los Angeles Kings and Chicago Blackhawks.
- Played in six All-Star games (1969–74).
- Was Second Team All-Star on defence, 1971–72 through 1973–74.
- Suffered a neck injury during 1976 playoffs that forced him to retire.
- Was interim coach of Chicago Blackhawks in 1976–77.
- Later returned to coach the Toronto Marlboros.

Memorable Quotes

So much has been said about the 1972 Canada-Russia series, but some comments just stand out. In closing, here are a select few that really encapsulate what happened at that great event.

"This was the greatest series played in *any* sport. This was war!"   — *Don Cherry*

"What Team Canada '72 accomplished was incredible. There has never been a greater victory in any sport."
— *Bobby Orr*

"This was a cold war. Our way of living against their way of living."   — *Rod Seiling*

"It wasn't a game anymore. It was society against society."
— *Phil Esposito*

"This is really life and death here. Down on that ice it is just sheer war."   — *Foster Hewitt*

"If we didn't win, it would be a mark for the rest of our lives."   — *Frank Mahovlich*

"It scared the hell out of me that I would have killed them to win. That scared me."   — *Phil Esposito*

"The greatest emotional moment a player can have is when he is standing on the ice surface in a foreign country and they are playing your national anthem."   — *Bobby Clarke*

"Nothing in hockey ever brought me so low or took me so high. And nothing meant so much."   — *Ken Dryden*

"I believe the biggest highlight of my hockey career was in 1972 when we were able to win that series that became so important to hockey."   — *Peter Mahovlich*

"There'll never be another one like it and I was proud to be a part of it."   — *Tony Esposito*

"I've never been prouder of a bunch of guys in my life. That team had a lot of heart."   — *Gary Bergman*

"Regardless of all the tension, these games contributed to establishing more human, more normal relations between people. The '72 series was absolutely one of the most brilliant events in world hockey in the twentieth century."

— *Vladimir Putin*, president of Russia

Index

Notes: The abbreviation PH in subheadings refers to Paul Henderson.
The letter "p" before a page number means "photo page".

227, 228, 237–38; with Toros,
p12, 116, 117–18, 125, 241
Henderson, Paul, post-hockey
career: as broker, 152; Power
to Change and LIG, 175–78;
seminary training, 156–57
Henderson, Paul, relationships:
marriage, 11, 156; with
Eleanor, 8–12, 153–56, 193,
194, 204, 230, 232; with
parents, 3–6, 12–14
Henderson, Paul, spiritual life:
becomes Christian, 114, 118,
156, 162–68, 171–72;
discontent after Summit Series,
159–61; and Eleanor, 165–66,
172–75, 177; enters seminary,
156–57; help to others,
142–43 (*see also Chapter
Fourteen*); life as a journey,
118; Power to Change and
LIG, 175–78, 243; purpose
statement, 157; roots, 159–62
Henderson, William (grand-father), 2
Heritage Hockey, 247
Heritagehockey.com, 245
Hershey, Pennsylvania, 27
Hershiser, Orel, 169
Hewitt, Foster, 90, 100, 275
Hockey Hall of Fame: Armstrong,
50; Mikita, 76; PH not in,
226–27, 229, 244; Sittler, 51;
Team of the Century, 226;
Ullman, 35
Hockey Night in Canada, 12, 13,
45, 273
Hodge, Ken, 18, 240
Holtz, Lou, 169
Horton, Tim, 48, 139–40
Horvath, Bronco, 26
Houle, Rejean, 121
Howald, Harold, p1
Howard, Glenn, 98
Howard, Russ, 98
Howe, Gordie: in WHA, 121, 129;
salary, 137–38; skill and
toughness, 136–37, 145; with

Red Wings, 34–35, 42, 135
Howe, Mark, p13, 122, 129
Howe, Marty, 122, 137
Hull, Bobby, 35, 58, 121, 129, 136
Hull, Dennis: Henderson Jersey
Homecoming Tour, 219; in
Summit Series, 65, 66, 80;
profile, 261–62; with St.
Catharines Teepees, 18
Hunter, Bob, 14
Hunter, Murray, 14

Imlach, George "Punch", 39–40,
43, 46–47, 139
Indianapolis Racers, 128
Inman, Robert, 190
International Hockey League, 43
International Ice Hockey Federation
(IIHF), 56, 229–30

Jarvis, Doug, 168
Jarvis, Wes, 168
Jeffrey, Larry, 25
Johnston, Eddie, 58, 71, 262

Keelor, Greg, 98, 99
Keller, Adam, 27
Kelly, Leonard Patrick "Red", 119
Keon, Dave, 45, 49, 50, 58, 129
Kharlamov, Valeri, 65, 82, 83
Kincardine, Ontario, 1–2, 219, 235
Kinnear, Guy, 144
Kirk, Gavin, 171
Kompalla, Josef, 88

Laforge, Claude, 27
Lajoie, Roger, 106
Landry, Tom, 169
Langway, Rod, 128
Lapointe, Guy, 58, 65, 262–63
LeaderImpact Group (LIG), 175,
185, 198, 243
Legendsofhockey.net, 245
Leger, Gilles, 125
Lemieux, Mario, 136, 221
Ley, Rick, 45, 114
Lindsay, Ted, 34, 35, 135, 145